A Transdiagnostic Approach to Develop Organization, Attention and Learning Skills

A Transdiagnostic Approach to Develop Organization, Attention and Learning Skills introduces the GOALS program—an innovative and skill-based approach that addresses the unique array of academic, occupational, and socio-emotional difficulties commonly faced by college students with underdeveloped executive functions.

This program consists of ten sessions delivered in a group format to help college students improve their academic performance. Over the course of these sessions, participants learn strategies to prioritize tasks and assignments; schedule and manage life responsibilities; cope with life stressors; identify relevant on-campus resources; prepare for upcoming exams; take well-structured notes; maintain motivation; and several other strategies designed to reach their academic goals. Each session builds on earlier sessions, so previously learned skills lay the foundation for the successful implementation of newly learned skills. This practical and easy-to-implement program includes detailed session notes for group leaders and reproducible handouts for participants including in-session activities, session summaries, and homework assignments.

This treatment manual is an essential resource for mental health providers who deliver interventions to students enrolled in post-secondary institutions pursuing undergraduate or graduate level degrees.

Laura K. Hansen, PhD is a Licensed Clinical Psychologist and Director of Clinical Psychology at Mitchell's Place, a clinic for children and adolescents with Neurodevelopmental Disorders in Birmingham, Alabama.

Brandi M. Ellis, PhD is a Clinical Psychology Postdoctoral Fellow at the University of Alabama at Birmingham, a Maternal and Child Health Leadership Education in Neurodevelopmental and Related Disabilities (LEND) training site.

Stephanie D. Smith, PhD is an Associate Professor of Psychology at the University of Southern Mississippi and Adjunct Faculty at the Yale Child Study Center.

A Transdiagnostic Approach to Develop Organization, Attention and Learning Skills

The GOALS Treatment Manual for College Students

Laura K. Hansen, PhD, Brandi M. Ellis, PhD, and
Stephanie D. Smith, PhD

Routledge
Taylor & Francis Group

NEW YORK AND LONDON

Cover image: © Getty Images

First published 2023
by Routledge
605 Third Avenue, New York, NY 10158

and by Routledge
4 Park Square, Milton Park, Abingdon, Oxon, OX14 4RN

Routledge is an imprint of the Taylor & Francis Group, an informa business

© 2023 Laura K. Hansen, Brandi M. Ellis and Stephanie D. Smith

The right of Laura K. Hansen, Brandi M. Ellis and Stephanie D. Smith to be identified as authors of this work has been asserted in accordance with sections 77 and 78 of the Copyright, Designs and Patents Act 1988.

Library of Congress Cataloguing-in-Publication Data
A catalog record for this title has been requested

ISBN: 978-1-032-05877-1 (hbk)
ISBN: 978-1-032-05876-4 (pbk)
ISBN: 978-1-003-19961-8 (ebk)

DOI: 10.4324/9781003199618

Typeset in Times New Roman
by MPS Limited, Dehradun

Contents

About the Authors

Laura K. Hansen, PhD is the Director of Clinical Psychology at Mitchell's Place, a special needs clinic serving the greater Birmingham community. She graduated from The University of Southern Mississippi in 2019 following the completion of a pre-doctoral internship in Clinical Psychology at Indiana University School of Medicine. She also completed a pediatric psychology postdoctoral fellowship at Children's Mercy Hospital in Kansas City, where she received the Edward Christophersen Award for Excellence in Child/Pediatric Psychology. Dr. Hansen has worked clinically with children, adolescents, and young adults with ADHD and related disorders since 2011. Dr. Hansen was a primary author of the initial GOALS treatment manual and was a group leader for the first two GOALS treatment sequences to obtain pilot data and feedback from group members regarding the program's effectiveness, feasibility, and acceptability.

Brandi M. Ellis, PhD is a clinical psychology postdoctoral fellow at The University of Alabama at Birmingham, a Maternal and Child Health Leadership Education in Neurodevelopmental and Related Disabilities (LEND) training site. Her current fellowship involves conducting research to improve treatment and assessment services of children, adolescents, and young adults with Neurodevelopmental Disorders including ADHD. She graduated from The University of Southern Mississippi in 2020 following the completion of a LEND Fellowship and a Pre-Doctoral Internship in Clinical Child and Pediatric Psychology at The University of Alabama at Birmingham. Dr. Ellis has worked clinically with children, adolescents, and young adults with ADHD and related disorders since 2015. She was a primary author on the initial GOALS treatment manual and was a group leader for the first three GOALS treatment sequences during which pilot data were collected to evaluate the program's effectiveness.

Stephanie D. Smith, PhD is an Associate Professor of Psychology at The University of Southern Mississippi and an Adjunct Assistant Professor at the Yale Child Study Center. She is the director of the Childhood Neurodevelopmental Disorders Lab at USM and has extensive experience conducting treatment outcome research with children and adolescents with Neurodevelopmental Disorders for the past 15 years. She has published over 25 peer-reviewed research papers in top-tier journals evaluating risk factors and treatments of ADHD and related disorders and her program of research has been funded by the Institute of Education Sciences, Brain and Behavior Research Foundation, and the National Institutes of Health. Dr. Smith is the senior author of the GOALS Treatment Manual and served as the clinical supervisor and principal investigator of the pilot study evaluating the effectiveness of the program presented in this manual.

▇ Introduction

Case Example

Leah is a 19-year-old student at a 4-year university. She is majoring in Biology and hoped to be accepted into the Nursing School program in her junior year of college. Leah sought out therapy services in the spring semester of her sophomore year after she was rejected from Nursing School. During her intake appointment, Leah reveals to her clinician that she has always had trouble managing her time and staying organized. In high school, Leah was an athlete and able to stay on-task and motivated to complete her school assignments because she had one-on-one tutoring and weekly check-in meetings with her coach. Since starting college, Leah has tried to schedule her classes three days a week so she can work two days a week and reserve her weekends for studying. However, she often finds that it is difficult to balance coursework and social engagements on the weekends, leading to frequent "cram" sessions on Sunday nights. Often, her notes from class are incomplete and she must track down notes from other students to study for tests, only to find that she does not have enough time to review all the material. Leah also noted that large projects (such as a recent term paper) are especially challenging, considering she waits until a few days before the due date to begin the project and does not have time to edit and review the assignment before she submits it to her course instructor.

Moreover, Leah finds it challenging to balance academic and work obligations while also enjoying time with her friends and family. She works part-time in the library on campus and was recently reprimanded by her boss for showing up late on too many occasions. Last week, Leah forgot she was scheduled for a shift and her co-worker had to text her a reminder. When she is at work, Leah's mind often wanders, and she sometimes shelves books in the wrong section because she is not paying close attention to details. She is worried that she will lose her job if things do not improve.

Because of these recent setbacks, Leah frequently feels stressed and does not know how to cope with these feelings. According to Leah, her rejection from the Nursing School program was because she turned in her application late and failed to include some of the required materials. Ultimately, Leah wants to figure out ways to manage her time more effectively, so she does well in her courses, keeps her job, and enjoys her time in college.

Leah's case demonstrates some of the struggles college students may face when expected to juggle a myriad of competing commitments at a time when the level of structure and support received in

DOI: 10.4324/9781003199618-1

high school is no longer available. Evolutionarily, humans have learned how to manage such commitments through the development of an intricate neural network of cognitive processes known as executive functions. However, the brain structures and myelination of neural pathways underlying executive functions are still developing as students enter and progress through college (Grieve et al., 2014). College students with psychological disorders that are commonly linked to executive dysfunction (e.g., Attention-Deficit/Hyperactivity Disorder, ADHD; Specific Learning Disorders, SLD; and Autism Spectrum Disorder, ASD) are thought to have a "double-deficit" because they must navigate the challenges associated with their disorder when their neural networks supporting EFs are still maturing (Fleming & McMahon, 2012). As in Leah's case, these students are often at increased risk of getting placed on academic probation, withdrawing from a greater number of classes, taking longer to complete their degrees, and dropping out before graduating (Barkley et al., 2008; National Center for Education Statistics, 2009). Further, self-management (e.g., goal setting, planning, task initiation, task completion, and study skills) and self-advocacy (e.g., effective communication with instructors; identification and use of school resources) skills have often been cited by students seeking accommodations while in college as vital for their success (Getzel & Thoma, 2008). Thus, there is a great need for interventions aimed at building such skills to offset executive function deficits in order to improve the academic success, retention, and graduation rates of these at-risk students.

The **G**roup for **O**rganization, **A**ttention and **L**earning **S**kills (GOALS) program outlined in this treatment manual has been specifically designed to meet this need. It has been modeled after other evidence-based Organizational Skills Training (OST) interventions for adolescents and adults with ADHD with vital modifications and enhancements to address the unique constellation of academic, emotional, occupational, and social needs of college students with executive function deficits. As part of this development process, we carefully reviewed the most recent and relevant research literature to identify executive functions shown to be under-developed across psychological disorders that have high prevalence rates among college students. We then incorporated skills into the GOALS program that have been theorized or empirically tested to circumvent the behavioral manifestations of these executive function deficits. The following section defines executive functions and how they should be conceptualized; what problems they may cause college students when underdeveloped; and suggested strategies to address these problems.

The Essentials of Executive Functions

Executive functions are higher-order cognitive processes underlying goal-directed behavior that have a profound influence on all aspects of daily living, especially with respect to a person's ability to learn, problem-solve, plan, and perform everyday tasks and activities (Kornell & Metcalfe, 2006). These cognitive processes are housed in the prefrontal cortex and regulate behaviors associated with problem-solving and attentional control (Dvorsky & Langberg, 2019). An important aspect of executive functions is that they are effortful (Diamond, 2013). In other words, the ability to pay attention, stop an already occurring behavior, or change an approach to solve a problem does not happen automatically and only strengthens with age and practice. There is a general consensus in the research literature that three core executive functions exist: inhibitory control, working memory, and cognitive flexibility (Diamond, 2013; Doebel, 2020). The GOALS program was developed to teach skills that compensate for executive function deficits so their behavioral manifestations (e.g., procrastination, missing deadlines, and inadequate study skills) are minimized and overall functioning (e.g., academic, social, and occupational) is improved.

Inhibitory Control

One primary executive function is inhibitory control, which refers to the ability to modulate behaviors, thoughts, emotions, or attention in response to internal or external stimuli. Essentially, inhibitory control allows for the stopping of an ongoing behavior so there is time to think through alternative options, thus lessening the occurrence of an impulsive or in-appropriate response (Diamond, 2013). In addition, inhibitory control facilitates the transition between activities by stopping the allocation of attention from one stimulus and moving it to another stimulus. For example, if a student walks into class while texting with a friend, in-hibitory control is the mental tool that allows the student to focus on the lecture instead of responding to every text message as it arrives.

Inhibitory control can be further subdivided into three distinct but related processes:

- ♦ **Attentional control** (sometimes called selective or focused attention) involves focusing on one stimulus while actively discounting other stimuli. Attentional control allows a student to focus on their instructor's voice while other students are having a whispered conversation in the row in front of them.
- ♦ **Cognitive inhibition** allows for the suppression of past experiences, memories, and thoughts that may intrude on directing attention to the present moment. Resistance to proactive interference (i.e., when information obtained in the past makes it difficult to learn something new) and retroactive interference (i.e., when information learned recently makes it difficult to remember what was previously learned) fall within the bounds of this mental process.
- ♦ **Self-control** is a complex aspect of inhibitory control. At its core, self-control is the ability to manage behaviors and emotions, even when presented with temptation. Relatedly, self-control is the mental process that makes staying focused and completing a task possible, rather than allowing distractions that are more interesting and entertaining get in the way.

Inhibitory control matures over time, so it is much less developed in children than in adolescents and adults (Diamond, 2013). Relatedly, inhibitory control in childhood appears to be linked to better outcomes in adulthood. For example, one longitudinal study followed girls through childhood into adolescence and found that inhibitory control was significantly associated with improved weight management, grades, cognitive functioning, and psychosocial well-being (Anzman-Frasca et al., 2015). Additionally, a large-scale research study found that inhibitory self-control in childhood was predictive of physical health, financial stability, decreased substance use, and fewer criminal offences in adolescence and early adulthood (Moffitt et al., 2011). These results suggest that inhibitory control influences several domains of functioning throughout de-velopment so that impairment of this cognitive process warrants intervention.

Difficulties with inhibitory control can have a significant impact on how students navigate the demands of college. For example, inhibitory control is necessary for persisting with the task-at-hand (e.g., listening to a class lecture) and not responding to distractions (e.g., reading an email as it is received). Inhibitory control also allows a student to discontinue an on-going activity to transition to a useful pursuit (e.g., stopping a conversation with a friend when class starts). These capabilities lay the foundation for more complex cognitive processes that allow for long-term planning and organization (Fleming & McMahon, 2012). To circumvent weaknesses in inhibitory control, the GOALS program teaches group members how to modify their environment to reduce distractions and practice exercises that strengthen their ability to focus on the present moment (i.e., mindfulness). Moreover, group members learn how to reward their efforts when they continue to work on mentally taxing tasks despite the presence of more tempting alternatives.

Working Memory

A second core executive function is working memory, or the capacity to hold information in mind after it is no longer perceived and manipulate it. It is further subdivided into verbal working memory and visual-spatial (nonverbal) working memory (Diamond, 2013). Working memory is required for a wide range of everyday tasks, from figuring out change at the gas station to reversing directions on a college campus to get back to a resident hall. More complex mental tasks, such as listening to a lecture, writing notes, and thinking about questions to ask the instructor, are also dependent on working memory. Thus, working memory is considered to underlie all tasks that require reasoning and creativity (Diamond, 2013).

Working memory and inhibitory control are related in that they are nearly always activated simultaneously when interacting with the environment. Essentially, inhibition allows for the halting of an ongoing or reactive behavioral response, and working memory allows for the formulation of a decision based on information presently held in mind. By considering the available data and using it to make an informed decision, it lessens the likelihood of an inhibitory error (Diamond, 2013). Moreover, inhibitory control supports working memory by allocating attention to the most important information while ignoring distractions and preventing the tendency to hyperfocus on one aspect of the situation.

Given the cross-cutting nature of working memory regarding its influence on several domains of functioning, a deficit in this area can be quite detrimental for students pursuing a postsecondary degree. For example, it has been found that a weakness in verbal working memory is significantly related to lower grade point averages among college students (Gropper & Tannock, 2009). College students with working memory impairment may have difficulty with processing the complex information they learn in class and encoding it into long-term memory. Additionally, less salient information, like assignment due dates or a course instructor's office hours, may be pushed out of working memory and forgotten. Thus, the GOALS program has incorporated strategies to address these challenges including how to actively listen, schedule using a planner or calendar, and employ memory rehearsal tools to store information (Fleming & McMahon, 2012).

Cognitive Flexibility

Cognitive flexibility, the third core executive function, refers to the ability to think flexibly to solve problems, process information, and make decisions. For example, cognitive flexibility allows for the prioritization of tasks and the adjustment of plans when demands change or new opportunities arise. Cognitive flexibility is also vital for interpersonal effectiveness, which involves both perspective taking and adaptability in social situations (Diamond, 2013). Thus, other commonly recognized executive functions (e.g., set shifting and attentional switching) are subsumed under this larger cognitive flexibility umbrella.

As cognitive flexibility develops later than the other two core executive functions (Diamond, 2013), it is particularly relevant to college students who often enter college in early adulthood when this higher-order mental process is still maturing. In fact, prior studies have revealed that cognitive flexibility is linked to better academic performance in reading, math, and writing, and overall grade point averages among college students (e.g., Kercood et al., 2017; Toraman et al., 2020). It has also been found to be associated with higher life quality, including students' satisfaction with their school climate and faculty members (Kercood et al., 2017). Interestingly, cognitive flexibility has been shown to be related to higher self-esteem and self-efficacy in a sample of Asian-American college students (Kim & Omizo, 2005). These results suggest that cognitive flexibility is important for positive college outcomes across a variety of functional domains.

In sum, cognitive flexibility plays a critical role in goal setting, planning, task prioritization, and resource allocation to facilitate the execution of tasks and long-term projects. College students with weaknesses in this area may struggle to balance their academic, occupational, and social obligations without becoming distressed or overwhelmed. They may also be more vulnerable to academic failure due to less developed mathematic, reading, and writing skills. Importantly, the GOALS program equips group members with self-management (e.g., goal setting, planning, and study skills) and self-advocacy skills (e.g., interpersonal effectiveness and identification of school resources) as well as coping strategies so they are better prepared to navigate the many challenges of college.

Table A.1 Core Executive Functions, Behavioral Manifestations of Impairment, and Strategies to Address Impairment

Executive Function		Example of Impairment	Strategies to Address Impairment
Inhibitory Control	Attentional control	Difficulty focusing on a homework assignment when others are talking	Reduce distracting stimuli by studying in a quiet place or putting in headphones
	Cognitive inhibition	Trouble attending to new material presented during a course lecture	Practice mindfulness—refocus attention to the present moment
	Self-control	Inability to persist with work when a favorite TV show is available to binge watch	Deliver contingent self-reward only after the task is accomplished or working for a pre-established time period
Working Memory	Verbal	Trouble listening and extracting important information from a course lecture	Apply active listening strategies & practice capturing content in note form

(Continued)

Table A.1 (Continued)

Executive Function		Example of Impairment	Strategies to Address Impairment
	Visual-spatial	Struggle to remember complex diagrams from assigned course readings	Rehearse new information in a different way to promote long-term memory encoding (e.g., describe it to a friend)
Cognitive Flexibility	Perspective-taking	Demands of a course do not coincide with expectations so grade is negatively impacted	Effectively communicate with instructor to achieve a better understanding of how to prepare for the evaluative components of a course
	Set shifting	Difficulty finding time to complete a class assignment when the due date is changed and overlaps with a social commitment	Prioritization of tasks and scheduling using a planner

Current Treatments for Executive Dysfunction
Academic Accommodations and Medication

Treatment options for college students with executive dysfunction are limited and less studied than treatments for adults at later stages of development. Academic accommodations (e.g., alternate exam formats, extended test-taking time, distraction-free testing environment, and classroom notetakers) is one option available to students if documentation is provided to their university verifying the presence of a disability; however, the benefits of these accommodations have not been rigorously tested and tend to only be seen when other forms of treatment are already in place (Lewandowski et al., 2013; Miller et al., 2015). Medication is another option for some students with executive function deficits (e.g., ADHD); however, few studies have evaluated the efficacy of medication in college students, especially with respect to their impact on executive functions and functional impairment (e.g., academic, social, and occupational). There is some evidence to suggest that certain stimulant medications (e.g., lisdexamfetamine) significantly improve symptoms of inattention and verbal working memory in college students (DuPaul et al., 2012), yet significant impairment in these domains remained after treatment in comparison to healthy controls. A few studies have also revealed that students taking stimulant medication for ADHD do not significantly differ on measures of academic performance (i.e., grade point averages, GPA) relative to their unmedicated peers (Advokat et al., 2011; Rabiner et al., 2009a). Given that stimulant medications are ineffective or result in side effects in up to 50% of adults with ADHD coupled with the increased risk of medication misuse (i.e., selling or sharing medication with others; Hartung et al., 2013) among college students, it has been suggested that medication should not be the first line of treatment for these students.

Cognitive Behavioral Interventions

An alternative or adjunct to these treatment options is OST interventions, which have shown a great deal of promise in significantly improving symptoms of inattention, organizational skills, and academic functioning in children, adolescents, and adults with ADHD (e.g., Langberg et al., 2008; 2012; Evans et al., 2004, 2005; Solanto et al., 2010, 2008). These OST interventions often comprise of shared elements including psychoeducation for ADHD; goal setting; time management; organization of materials and workspaces; use of calendar systems for scheduling; prioritization of tasks; planning of long-term projects; and contingent self-rewards to enhance motivation (see Langberg et al., 2008 for a review). There are a handful of treatment manuals available to mental health providers who deliver therapy services to adult clients with ADHD struggling with executive dysfunction, particularly with temporal planning and organization. *Mastering Your Adult ADHD: A Cognitive Behavioral Program* by Safren et al. (2017) is a cognitive behavioral intervention for adults with ADHD and includes three core modules covering the establishment of systems for keeping track of appointments and tasks, reducing distractibility, and improving adaptive thinking skills. There are two optional modules that present strategies to combat procrastination and ways to involve family members in treatment for additional support and accountability. In the initial study evaluating the efficacy of this intervention (Safren et al., 2005), the treatment group outperformed the control group on clinician and self-reported ratings of ADHD symptoms. Further, a significantly greater number of participants in the treatment group (56%) were rated by clinicians as treatment responders than participants in the control group (13%). Another study compared this intervention to relaxation-based therapy with educational support in medicated adults with ADHD who still had residual symptoms (Safren et al., 2010). Results were similar to the findings from the initial efficacy study as both clinician and self-reported ADHD symptoms significantly improved post-treatment and there were more treatment responders for the cognitive behavioral intervention than the relaxation-based therapy. These studies offer empirical support that OST interventions within a cognitive behavioral framework ameliorate ADHD symptomatology; however, it is unclear whether organizational skills were indeed learned and internalized or how symptom reduction translates to improvements in executive functions or functional impairment.

Another treatment manual, *The Cognitive-Behavioral Therapy for Adult ADHD: An Integrative Psychosocial and Medical Approach*, co-authored by Ramsay and Rostain (2014) outlines the content of 20 individual psychotherapy sessions that aim to develop coping strategies for the management of ADHD symptoms and assist with the recognition and adjustment of maladaptive thoughts and beliefs. ADHD psychoeducation as well as organizational and time management components are also part of this treatment. In an open-trial study evaluating a treatment approach that combined this intervention with stimulant medication in a sample of adults with ADHD, it was found that there was a significant and positive change for self-rated ADHD symptoms and clinician-rated ADHD symptom severity and overall functioning (Rostain & Ramsay, 2006). Although these results are promising, it is impossible to disentangle the effects of the two interventions and determine which contributed the most to these improved outcomes. Unlike the GOALS program, neither treatment manual was designed with college students in mind; therefore, specific strategies (e.g., structured note-taking, test preparation, effective communication with instructors, and identification of on-campus resources) aimed at circumventing the executive dysfunction that impact the learning and success of college students are not included.

Over the past decade, Solanto and colleagues have been evaluating and refining a cognitive behavioral intervention for adult ADHD, which was designed to build executive self-management skills inclusive of time management, organization, and planning in a group format. Their treatment manual, *Cognitive-Behavioral Therapy for Adult ADHD: Targeting Executive Dysfunction* (Solanto, 2011), has been evaluated via studies using open trial and randomized controlled trial designs, which have revealed large to small treatment effects on measures of inattention and organizational skills where the magnitude of the effect size depended upon the study design (Solanto et al., 2008, 2010).

More recently, they have adapted their treatment protocol, so it more adequately aligns with the needs of college students with ADHD. Specifically, students are taught how to identify and use resources on campus; read to retain information; listen to lectures and take notes; and write and edit term papers. The organizational, time management, and planning skills were also updated so they were relevant to the academic routines of college students while taking into consideration the on-campus distractions that may impede student progress. In a recent study evaluating the effectiveness of this intervention, a total of 15 students completed at least 9 of the 12 two-hour sessions, and 39% of students who received treatment no longer met diagnostic criteria for adult ADHD at the time of study completion (Solanto & Scheres, 2020). There was also a significant improvement on measures assessing inattention (clinician and self-rated), executive functions, and learning strategies; however, students' GPA remained unchanged from pre- to post-treatment. Overall, these results offer initial evidence of the effectiveness of this intervention in reducing symptoms of inattention and executive function deficits that are known to negatively impact the functioning of students with ADHD at the college level.

Effectiveness of the GOALS Program

Two major distinguishing features of the GOALS program relative to the previously reviewed treatment manuals is that it was specifically developed for college students with executive dysfunction and may be used with students across diagnostic categories. It is intended to be delivered in a group format and takes a skill-based behavioral approach to promote skill internalization. As cognitive restructuring is not embedded in the treatment sequence, it requires less of a time commitment from group members (90 minutes for ten weeks vs. 120 minutes for 12 weeks). Importantly, a pilot efficacy study of the GOALS program involving thirty-three students who completed the entirety of the program revealed clinically significant improvements in measures assessing executive functions, learning strategies, and symptoms of inattention (Smith et al., in preparation). Furthermore, anonymous feedback surveys indicated that students had a high level of satisfaction with the program and found it to be extremely useful. Studies evaluating the GOALS program's impact on an objective measure of sustained attention and response inhibition and students' academic performance are currently underway.

Implementation of the GOALS Program

Purpose and Structure of the GOALS Program

Who Should Participate?

The GOALS program was developed for college students with significant impairment in executive functions across diagnostic categories (e.g., ADHD, SLD, and ASD). As mentioned previously, the GOALS program follows a similar approach to OST for children and adolescents with ADHD (e.g., *Homework, Organization, and Planning Skills (HOPS) Intervention*, Langberg, 2011; *Organizational Skills Training for Children with ADHD*, Gallagher et al., 2014), and draws on behavioral and cognitive-behavioral based interventions for adults with ADHD (e.g., *Cognitive-Behavioral Therapy for Adult ADHD*; Solanto, 2011). However, the GOALS program is innovative in that it is a skill-based approach implemented in a group format, which was developed to address the unique academic, emotional, occupational, and social difficulties of students (ages 18 and above) with executive dysfunction who are enrolled in college-level courses. While the program was initially developed for young adults just beginning college, the skills taught throughout this program are relevant and applicable to college students at different stages in their academic careers (e.g., undecided freshman, sophomore majoring in anthropology, and master's student in journalism). In fact, this intervention has been successfully implemented with students at both the undergraduate and graduate level. Importantly, skills are taught and applied in a manner that sets students up for academic success, and once mastered, these skills readily extend to life beyond the college setting.

Basic Manual Structure

Over the course of 10, 90-minute sessions, GOALS group members are taught various organizational and learning skills with the ultimate objective of improving their academic performance. Each session builds on past sessions so previously learned skills lay the foundation for the successful implementation of newly learned skills. For example, group members begin by learning how to build motivation, increase time awareness, and prioritize and schedule tasks. These skills are eventually combined to learn and implement more complex organizational strategies such as planning and completing a long-term project. It is recommended that no more than one group session is held per week, as this schedule allows sufficient time for group members to learn and practice new skills. Each session usually covers more than one skill so having multiple group sessions per week puts a greater demand on group members, which may increase the likelihood of treatment noncompliance or early termination. Each session should be at least 90 minutes, as this session length allows sufficient time for group discussion as well as skill demonstration and practice, which are critical components of the GOALS program and necessary for skill internalization.

Each session follows the same basic structure. Group leaders begin with a review of the homework that was assigned during the previous session. Following homework review, new skills are presented using the GOALS teaching method—describe, demonstrate, and discuss. Specifically, group leaders introduce and describe the skills specific to that session; group members observe a demonstration of these skills or practice the skills; and group members ask questions or discuss how they will apply these skills to real world situations. Each session ends with a review of the content covered, a discussion and assignment of homework, and a brief overview of the upcoming session. This structure allows for a balance between didactic training, discussion, and activities to facilitate learning and to ensure that group members remain engaged and motivated throughout the treatment process. Each session also emphasizes real-world application of skills to encourage generalizability beyond the group therapy setting. For example, weekly homework assignments are designed to make use of each skill while facilitating rather than adding to group members' already existing obligations. This important feature of the GOALS program contributes to group members' buy-in and treatment compliance, as it tends to alleviate stress surrounding the complexity of juggling multiple responsibilities.

Two skill review sessions are built into the program, one about midway through the treatment sequence (Session 6) and one at the very end of the treatment sequence (Session 10). These sessions give group members an opportunity to problem-solve any barriers preventing them from successfully implementing the skills taught in group. Group members' progress and successes are also highlighted and discussed during these review sessions.

The manual also includes fidelity checklists that assess to what extent the sessions' tasks have been accomplished by the group leaders. Group leaders are rated on a three-point Likert scale (*0 = Group Leader did not execute task; 1 = Group Leader partially executed task; 2 = Group Leader fully executed task*). Tasks include more general tasks, such as reviewing homework and telling group members the topic of upcoming sessions, and session-specific tasks. A treatment fidelity score of approximately 80% (score earned/total possible score × 100) reflects adequate delivery of the treatment manual.

Who Should Use the GOALS Program?

The GOALS program should be implemented by professionals with a training background in adult psychopathology and behavioral or cognitive behavioral interventions. Its intended audience are mental health providers, such as social workers, psychologists, psychiatrists, counselors, or practitioners-in-training (master-level or doctoral-level graduate students), who deliver interventions to young adults (ages 18+ years) enrolled in post-secondary institutions pursuing undergraduate or graduate level degrees. The GOALS program may be used in traditional outpatient settings for college students such as Student Counseling Centers or Psychology Training Clinics. It may also be used in the context of a class or student success initiative to provide at-risk college students on academic probation with the skills needed to graduate.

User's Guide for GOALS Treatment Manual

General Tips and Considerations

The GOALS Treatment Manual was designed to be user-friendly and inclusive of all materials needed to implement the program. Its layout is meant to guide group leaders through each session by providing visual anchors and cues to draw attention to important activities and concepts. The "*Quick Look*" section at the start of each session gives group leaders a concise overview of its content and flow. Group leaders may reference this section to quickly familiarize themselves with the session objectives, materials needed to deliver the session, and session highlights inclusive of skills that will be taught and homework that will be assigned. The

"*Detailed Session Content*" comes next and is further subdivided into three sections: check-in, skills introduction, and session wrap-up. Sessions start (check-in) with a review of the previous session content and a discussion of the assigned homework and ends (wrap-up) with a summary of the upcoming session and the distribution of homework that puts newly learned skills into practice. The main content of the session (skills introduction) follows the GOALS teaching method and clearly outlines when and how a skill should be described, demonstrated, and discussed so group members are equipped to use the skill outside of session.

The GOALS Treatment Manual is not intended to be recited verbatim but instead group leaders should paraphrase the content using a conversational style, so sessions are engaging and promote interaction among group members. Thus, group leaders should familiarize themselves with the content presented in each session and deliver it to group members in a way that is relatable and relevant to them. For example, the manual gives examples to further explain how skills are used and offers questions to prompt group discussion; however, group leaders are encouraged to expand upon, add to, and substitute these suggestions as they see fit. As group leaders get to know group members, it is expected that they will share their experiences navigating the challenges of college and how they apply skills learned in group to their everyday life and this should be encouraged. Although there is a great deal of flexibility with respect to implementing the GOALS program, group leaders must adhere to the GOALS teaching method and provide a rationale for why each skill should be used and under what circumstances; explain how skills build on and connect to other skills; and offer instruction on how to implement each skill. We have included fidelity checklists for each session to evaluate how well group leaders adhere to the main tenets of the session content, which is especially useful when group leaders are first learning how to deliver the GOALS program. It is recommended that two group leaders run a GOALS group where one has previous experience implementing the program or a similar group-based intervention, which will assist with the training of the more junior group leader and help maintain the integrity of the program.

The appendices that accompany each session provide group leaders with the materials needed to run in-session activities and to facilitate the assignment and completion of homework. Session outlines and homework worksheets are standard handouts for every session. Depending upon the session content, additional handouts are provided to review or give further detail about complex skills (e.g., Extracting Vital Information from a Course Syllabus) or to inform group members of resources that may be beneficial to them (e.g., Accessing Accommodations). The handouts required for each session are listed in the "*Quick Look*" section and should be printed for distribution to group members prior to the start of each session.

The Importance of Outlining Expectations

Session 1 of the GOALS Treatment Manual is intended to orient group members to what should be anticipated from the program and group leaders. It also serves as a way for group leaders to clearly communicate expectations to group members who participate in the GOALS program. Establishing clear expectations is essential to running a successful group, as it outlines how group members should conduct themselves to get the most out of the program and sets the precedent as to why certain problematic behaviors need to be addressed or may result in unfavorable consequences if not remedied (e.g., expulsion from the group). Expectations regarding electronic device use, respectful participation, attendance, confidentiality, and preparedness for group meetings should be thoroughly discussed and agreed upon by group members, and any questions regarding expectations should be clarified. The expectations for homework completion are especially important and warrant special attention. Homework assignments are designed to provide group members with intentional, semi-structured practice of newly learned skills. This practice helps group members identify strategies that were successful or unsuccessful in implementing these skills. When homework is completed in a timely manner, any challenges group members encountered with skill use can be problem-solved with group leaders and group members during the homework review portion of sessions.

Building the Intervention Group and Tracking Progress

Based on our experience implementing GOALS, an ideal number of group members is about six to eight participants, as this group size allows for adequate discussion and skills practice during each session. However, sessions may be conducted with as few as two participants and as many as ten participants. As this program was developed for college students with executive function deficits who are struggling academically, it is imperative that the GOALS program is an appropriate fit for group members. For example, a potential group member may have a pressing mental health concern (e.g., suicidality, psychosis, trauma, or aggression) that is better served by an evidence-based intervention known to effectively treat that symptom profile. In such cases, group leaders will need to carefully consider whether potential group members should be referred for individual therapy to focus on that presenting concern or if they may simultaneously participate in the GOALS program and individual therapy.

Given the complexities of determining fit to the GOALS program, it is recommended that a thorough intake assessment is completed before enrolling potential participants into the program. A broad clinical interview such as the *Structured Clinical Interview for DSM-5 - Clinician Version* (SCID-5-CV; First et al., 2016) will allow for the formulation of a diagnostic impression and assist in determining treatment needs. A thorough medical, developmental, and psychological history should be taken, as not all factors contributing to academic problems or executive dysfunction may be captured by the SCID-5-CV (e.g., some Neurodevelopmental Disorders such as SLD). The GOALS program strives to address the behavioral manifestations of executive dysfunction (e.g., procrastination, missed deadlines, and inadequate study skills) by teaching skills that may prevent or circumvent the negative academic outcomes associated with these behaviors. Therefore, psychometrically sound measures that assess executive functions (e.g., *Behavior Rating Inventory of Executive Function - Adult Version,* Roth et al., 2005; *Barkley Deficits in Executive Functioning Scale*, Barkley, 2011) as well as organizational and learning skills (e.g., *Learning and Study Strategies Inventory - 3rd Edition*, Weinstein et al., 2016) will determine the starting level of impairment of group members and highlight what skills should be focused on during treatment. They may also be used as treatment progress measures and will inform group leaders if repeating certain sessions is necessary.

References

Advokat, C., Lane, S.M., & Luo, C. (2011). College students with and without ADHD: Comparison of self-report of medication usage, study habits, and academic achievement. *Journal of Attention Disorders, 15*(8), 656–666.

Anzman-Frasca, S., Francis, L.A., & Birch, L.L. (2015). Inhibitory control is associated with psychosocial, cognitive, and weight outcomes in a longitudinal sample of girls. *Translational Issues in Psychological Science, 1*, 203.

Barkley, R.A. (2012). *Executive functions: What they are, how they work, and why they evolved.* Guilford Press.

Barkley, R.A. (2011). *Barkley Deficits in Executive Functioning Scale (BDEFS for Adults)*. Guilford Press.

Barkley, R.A., Murphy, K.R., & Fischer, M. (2008). *ADHD in adults: What the science says*. Guilford Press.

Diamond, A. (2013). Executive functions. *Annual Review of Psychology*, *64*, 135–168.

Doebel, S. (2020). Rethinking Executive function and its development. *Perspectives on Psychological Science,* 15, 942–956.

DuPaul, G.J., Weyandt, L.L., Rossi, J.S., Vilardo, B.A., O'Dell, S.M., Carson, K.M., ... & Swentosky, A. (2012). Double-blind, placebo-controlled, crossover study of the efficacy and safety of lisdexamfetamine dimesylate in college students with ADHD. *Journal of Attention Disorders*, *16*(3), 202–220.

Dvorsky, M.R., & Langberg, J.M. (2019). Predicting impairment in college students with ADHD: The role of executive functions. *Journal of Attention Disorders*, *23*, 1624–1636.

Evans, S.W., Axelrod, J., & Langberg, J. (2004). Efficacy of a school-based treatment program for middle school youth with ADHD. *Behavior Modification*, *28*(4), 528–547.

Evans, S.W., Langberg, J., Raggi, V.L., Allen, J., & Buvinger, E. (2005). Preliminary data from the school based treatment for you adolescents with ADHD. *Journal of Attention Disorders*, *9*, 343–353.

First, M.B., Williams, J.B.W., Karg, R.S., & Spitzer, R.L. (2016). *Structured Clinical Interview for DSM-5 Disorders-Clinician Version (SCID-5-CV)*. American Psychiatric Association.

Fleming, A.P., & McMahon, R.J. (2012). Developmental context and treatment principles for ADHD among college students. *Clinical Child and Family Psychology Review*, *15*, 303–329.

Gallagher, R., Abikoff, H.B., & Spira, E.G. (2014). *Organizational skills training for children with ADHD: An empirically supported treatment*. Guilford Publications.

Getzel, E.E., & Thoma, C.A. (2008). Experiences of college students with disabilities and the importance of self-determination in higher education settings. *Career Development for Exceptional Individuals*, *31*, 77–84.

Grieve, A., Webne-Behrman, L., Couillou, R., & Sieben-Schneider, J. (2014). Self-report assessment of executive functioning in college students with disabilities. *Journal of Postsecondary Education and Disability*, *27*, 19–32.

Gropper, R.J., & Tannock, R. (2009). A pilot study of working memory and academic achievement in college students with ADHD. *Journal of Attention Disorders*, *12*, 574–581.

Hartung, C.M., Canu, W.H., Cleveland, C.S., Lefler, E.K., Mignogna, M.J., Fedele, D.A.,... & Clapp, J.D. (2013). Stimulant medication use in college students: Comparison of appropriate users, misusers, and nonusers. *Psychology of Addictive Behaviors*, *27*(3), 832.

Kercood, S., Lineweaver, T.T., Frank, C.C., & Fromm, E.D. (2017). Cognitive flexibility and its relationship to academic achievement and career choice of college students with and without attention deficit hyperactivity disorder. *Journal of Postsecondary Education and Disability*, *30*(4), 329–344.

Kim, B.S., & Omizo, M.M. (2005). Asian and European American Cultural values, collective self-esteem, acculturative stress, cognitive flexibility, and general self-efficacy among Asian American College Students. *Journal of Counseling Psychology*, *52*, 412.

Kornell, N., & Metcalfe, J. (2006). Study efficacy and the region of proximal learning framework. *Journal of Experimental Psychology: Learning, Memory, and Cognition*, *32*, 609.

Langberg, J.M. (2011). *Improving children's homework, organization, and planning skills (HOPS)*. National Association of School Psychologists.

Langberg, J.M., Epstein, J.N., Becker, S.P., Girio-Herrera, E., & Vaughn, A.J. (2012). Evaluation of the homework, organization and planning skills (hops) intervention of middle school students with attention deficit hyperactivity disorder as implemented by school mental health providers. *School Psychology Review, 41*(3), 342–364.

Langberg, J.M., Epstein, J.N., & Graham, A.J. (2008). Organizational-skills interventions in the treatment of ADHD. *Expert Review of Neurotherapeutics, 8*(10), 1549–1561.

Langberg, J.M., Epstein, J.N., Urbanowicz, C.M., Simon, J.O., & Graham, A.J. (2008). Efficacy of organization skills intervention to improve the academic functioning of students with attention-deficit/hyperactivity disorder. *School Psychology Quarterly, 23*(3), 407–417.

Lewandowski, L., Gathje, R.A., Lovett, B.J., & Gordon, M. (2013). Test-taking skills in college students with and without ADHD. *Journal of Psychoeducational Assessment, 31*(1), 41–52.

Miller, L.A., Lewandowski, L.J., & Antshel, K.M. (2015). Effects of extended time for college students with and without ADHD. *Journal of Attention Disorders, 19*(8), 678–686.

Moffitt, T.E., Arseneault, L., Belsky, D., Dickson, N., Hancox, R.J., Harrington, H., Houts, R., Poulton, R., Roberts, B.W., Ross, S., Sears, M.R., Thomson, W.M., & Caspi, A. (2011). A gradient of childhood self-control predicts health, wealth, and public safety. *Proceedings of the National Academy of Sciences of the United States of America, 108,* 2693–2698. 10.1073/pnas.1010076108

National Center for Educational Statistics, United States. Office of Educational Research, Improvement. Center for Education Statistics, & Institute of Education Sciences (US). (2009). The condition of education. US Department of Education, Office of Educational Research and Improvement, National Center for Education Statistics.

Rabiner, D.L., Anastopoulos, A.D., Costello, E.J., Hoyle, R.H., McCabe, S.E., & Swartzwelder, H.S. (2009a). The misuse and diversion of prescribed ADHD medications by college students. *Journal of Attention Disorders, 13*(2), 144–153.

Ramsay, J.R., & Rostain, A.L. (2014). *Cognitive behavioral therapy for adult ADHD: An integrative psychosocial and medical approach.* Routledge.

Rostain, A.L., & Ramsay, J.R. (2006). A combined treatment approach for adults with ADHD—results of an open study of 43 patients. *Journal of Attention Disorders, 10,* 150–159.

Roth, R.M., Isquith, P.K., & Gioia, G.A. (2005). *Behavior Rating Inventory of Executive Function - Adult Version (BRIEF-A).* Psychological Assessment Resources.

Safren, S.A., Otto, M.W., Sprich, S., Winett, C.L., Wilens, T.E., & Biederman, J. (2005). Cognitive-behavioral therapy for ADHD in medication-treated adults with continued symptoms. *Behaviour Research and Therapy, 43*(7), 831–842.

Safren, S.A., Sprich, S.E., Mimiaga, M.J., Surman, C., Knouse, L., Groves, M., & Otto, M.W. (2010). Cognitive behavioral therapy vs. relaxation with educational support for medication-treated adults with ADHD and persistent symptoms: a randomized controlled trial. *JAMA, 304*(8), 875–880.

Safren, S.A., Sprich, S.E., Perlman, C.A., & Otto, M.W. (2017). *Mastering your adult ADHD: A cognitive-behavioral treatment program, therapist guide.* Oxford University Press.

Solanto, M.V. (2011). *Cognitive-behavioral therapy for adult ADHD: Targeting executive dysfunction.* The Guilford Press.

Solanto, M.V., Marks, D.J., Mitchell, K.J., Wasserstein, J., & Kofman, M.D. (2008). Development of a new psychosocial treatment for adult ADHD. *Journal of Attention Disorders, 11*(6), 728–736.

Solanto, M.V., Marks, D.J., Wasserstein, J., Mitchell, K., Abikoff, H., Alvir, J.M.J., & Kofman, M.D. (2010). Efficacy of meta-cognitive therapy for adult ADHD. *American Journal of Psychiatry*, *167*(8), 958–968.

Solanto, M.V., & Scheres, A. (2020). Feasibiliy, Acceptability, and Effectiveness of a New Cognitive-Behavioral Intervention for College Students with ADHD. *Journal of Attention Disorders*, 1–15. 10.1177/1087054720951865.

Toraman, Ç., Özdemir, H.F., Kosan, A.M.A., & Orakci, S. (2020). Relationships between cognitive flexibility, perceived quality of faculty life, learning approaches, and academic achievement. *International Journal of Instruction*, *13*(1), 85–100.

Weinstein, C.E., Palmer, D.R., & Acee, T.W. (2016). *Learning and Study Strategies Inventory-Third Edition (LASSI 3rd Edition)*. H&H Publishing Company, Inc.

Wolf, L.E. (2001). College students with ADHD and other hidden disabilities: Outcomes and interventions. *Annals of the New York Academy of Sciences*, *931*, 385–395.

Chapter 1

Introduction to the Goals Program

Quick Look

Objectives

♦ Group members will learn what the GOALS program entails, including the rationale for the program, learning objectives, summary of session content, and expectations for participation.

♦ Group members will learn how to define executive functions (EFs), where they are situated in the brain, and how less developed EFs may impact learning and organizational skills.

♦ Group members will receive a brief introduction to the concept of using contingent self-rewards to increase motivation for task initiation and completion.

Materials Needed

♦ Baseline Progress Measures (Optional)
♦ Appendix 1.1: Session 1 Outline
♦ Appendix 1.2: Executive Functions Psychoeducation (Handout)
♦ Appendix 1.3: Self-Rewards and Barriers to Success (Homework)
♦ GOALS Binder (recommended)
♦ *Optional:* Session 1 Fidelity Checklist (Table 1.1)

It is recommended that the group leaders provide each group member with a binder at the first session to organize GOALS-related materials (i.e., session notes, handouts, and homework assignments).

Session Highlights

♦ Introduction to GOALS & Session Format
  • Program overview and treatment rationale
  • Program learning objectives
  • Expectations and responsibilities
  • GOALS teaching method (describe, demonstrate, and discuss)

DOI: 10.4324/9781003199618-2

♦ Learn new skills
  • Executive functions psychoeducation
  • Contingent self-rewards
♦ Wrap-up
  • Assign homework (Self-Rewards & Barriers to Success)
  • Briefly introduce Session 2 content (Self-Advocacy & Building Motivation)

Detailed Session Content

Tip for Group Leaders: Progress measures are an optional component of the GOALS program. If group leaders have chosen to administer progress measures to group members and have not included these measures as part of the intake evaluations, additional time should be allotted at the beginning of this session for progress measures to be distributed and completed.

Describe the GOALS Program and Its Rationale

General Overview of the GOALS Program

Explain why group members are participating in the GOALS program and how they may benefit from it. Describe the role of group leaders and highlight the overarching learning objectives of the GOALS program.

Why Are Group Members Here?

Group members have either been self-referred or referred by someone who felt they could benefit from learning strategies (i.e., planning, organization, task initiation, and study skills) that are known to promote academic success.

Why Are Group Leaders Here?

Group leaders will help group members identify their strengths and potential areas for improvement. They will teach and develop skills that will capitalize on group members' abilities, so that they are successful inside and outside of the classroom.

Overall Program Objectives

♦ Teach group members how to plan and prioritize daily tasks including class-related assignments and obligations.

♦ Assist group members to develop coping and self-regulation skills in the face of stressful or challenging situations.

♦ Educate group members about how less developed executive functions may impact their learning and daily functioning. Help group members learn how to connect with resources that may be helpful in offsetting these difficulties.

♦ Provide group members with the tools necessary to become their own self-advocates including how to communicate effectively with others to achieve success in the classroom and workplace.

♦ Demonstrate to group members how to sustain motivation in their pursuit of short- and long-term goals through reinforcement and the visualization of more distant rewards.

Provide group members with a summary of the content covered in this session and upcoming sessions:

♦ **Session 1** (Introduction to the GOALS Program): This session serves as an introduction to the program and is didactic in format. Group members learn how the information will be presented and taught, as well as expectations to promote the effectiveness of the GOALS program. Session 1 is followed by nine 90-minute sessions that are more interactive as skills are actively taught and practiced.

♦ **Session 2** (Self-Advocacy and Building Motivation): Group members will learn how to locate campus resources and effectively communicate with course instructors to address any problems they may be having in class. They will be taught how to extract important information from their course syllabi so that important course deadlines are not missed. Finally, group members will learn how to properly use self-rewards to build and maintain their motivation to complete various tasks.

♦ **Session 3** (Taking Notes from Lectures and Course Readings): Group members will learn how to take thorough and helpful notes during class lectures, reading assignments, and other class-related activities. They will be taught how to actively listen during course lectures and presentations and how to take notes that capture the main themes and details of the course lectures and readings.

♦ **Session 4** (Time Awareness and Tuning Out Distractions): Group members will learn how to improve their time awareness, an essential skill that lays the foundation for strategies introduced later in the program (e.g., scheduling and planning long-term projects). Mindfulness will also be introduced and practiced during this session to improve group members' ability to tune out external distractions and focus on important tasks.

♦ **Session 5** (Prioritizing and Scheduling Tasks): Group members will learn how to create to-do lists, prioritize tasks, and make use of a planner. While these skills may seem simple and intuitive, they are essential for navigating the demands of college and maintaining a healthy work-life balance.

♦ **Session 6** (Program Review and Getting Organized): This session focuses on reviewing and reinforcing the skills taught in Sessions 1 through 5. Group members are given the opportunity to discuss the successes and challenges they faced while implementing these skills. Group members will also learn how to organize their workspace and course materials to enhance their productivity and focus.

♦ **Session 7** (Overcoming Procrastination and Coping with Stress): Group members will learn strategies to overcome procrastination and deal with stressors that may hinder their success. Skills to be covered in this session include how to initiate tasks, stay motivated to make progress, and use coping strategies when feeling overwhelmed.

♦ **Session 8** (Planning a Long-Term Project): Group members will learn how to plan a long-term project by breaking it down into smaller, more manageable tasks; prioritizing and ranking each task; and scheduling the completion of these tasks.

♦ **Session 9** (Studying for Tests of Varying Formats): Group members will learn how to prepare for tests of varying formats (i.e., multiple-choice vs. short answer/essay) using study strategies known to improve performance on exams and quizzes.

♦ **Session 10** (Summary of Program and Progress Made): This session essentially serves as group members' graduation from the program. Skills learned throughout the program will be reviewed and progress made by group members will be highlighted and discussed. Group members will be given the opportunity to ask questions about how they will apply and maintain the use of these skills in the future.

Expectations for the GOALS Program

Set clear expectations for group members at the first session so that benefits from the program are maximized and experiences of members can be shared in a safe environment.

♦ *Electronics:* Cell phones, laptops, tablets, and other electronic devices must be placed on silent mode and put away while group is in session. It is easy to become distracted by notifications, messages, and activities that are unrelated to group on such devices. Given that a significant amount of material is covered during each session, it is very important to limit these distractions.

♦ *Participation:* Group members are expected to be respectful of and polite to group leaders and fellow group members. Respectful participation means listening to the input of other group members without judgement and contributing to the discussion by asking relevant questions or elaborating upon (e.g., providing examples) content covered in the session.

♦ *Attendance:* It is recommended that group members attend a *minimum* of eight out of ten sessions to complete the program, as attendance is critical for the successful internalization of skills and preservation of the benefits of the group format (e.g., support from group members and sharing of information). It is also recommended that group members be required to contact group leaders 24 hours in advance if they cannot attend a session. In situations where multiple group members will be absent for a given meeting, it may be necessary to reschedule a session. Having adequate notice of absences allows group leaders to make such decisions and notify remaining group members in a timely fashion. Group sessions must begin on time considering there is a great deal of material to cover, and group members are expected to be present when the session begins.

♦ *Confidentiality:* What is said in group, stays in group. Confidentiality is vital to ensure the GOALS group is a safe place for members to candidly share information and seek help.

♦ *Preparedness:* Group members are expected to come to group prepared, meaning homework assignments are completed *prior* to the next group session. Homework assignments are designed to allow for the application of skills learned in group to real-world situations. Each session's homework review component also provides group members with the opportunity to share how they successfully implemented a skill and provides group leaders with the opportunity to problem-solve challenges group members faced when using a skill.

♦ *GOALS binders:* GOALS binders are meant to provide members with a means of keeping their program materials organized and secure in one place. Successful participation in each group session requires that group members bring their program materials, especially the previous session's homework, to each group meeting. Group members will learn how to organize course materials in Session 6 by applying this skill to the GOALS binder.

Explain How Skills Are Taught

Each session group leaders will teach skills designed to increase the likelihood of group members meeting their academic and life goals. The following approach will be used to teach skills and promote skill internalization:

♦ *Describe:* Define the skill and give examples of how the skill may be used
♦ *Demonstrate:* Practice implementing the skill through in-session activities
♦ *Discuss:* Ensure all group members understand the skill by soliciting examples from group members of how they might use the skill in real-world settings and allowing them to ask questions about the skill. The importance of practice will be emphasized so that group members understand that behavior change occurs slowly and skills will become second nature only through repeated use.

Executive Functions Psychoeducation

Distribute Appendix 1.2: Executive Functions Psychoeducation (Handout).

The Importance of Executive Functions

Executive functions are higher-order cognitive or mental processes that underlie goal-directed behavior and are orchestrated by the prefrontal cortex in the brain. They refer to abilities such as attentional control, working memory, planning, cognitive flexibility (i.e., the ability to think about things in different ways or problem-solve), and the self-regulation of emotions and behavior (Goldstein et al., 2014). Executive functions allow for the evaluation of a task or demand and the formulation of a plan to execute it. Thus, executive functions help us make informed decisions and respond to the environment in the best way possible. They are vital to our success across all domains of functioning (i.e., academic, occupational, and social).

These mental processes are not isolated to one area of the brain—rather, they are part of a network that work together to help us navigate the world. Sometimes, people struggle because one or more executive functions are not working optimally or as well as the others. By knowing how executive functions work, are coordinated in the brain, and how they impact daily functioning, it is possible to identify when there is a problem and how to address that problem.

Orbitofrontal Cortex

The orbitofrontal cortex helps control behaviors by inhibiting reactions to strong urges or feelings (Hooker & Knight, 2006). For example, it prevents a student from hitting someone when he/she is angry or blurting out random thoughts during a class lecture. The orbitofrontal cortex also helps stop behaviors that are already underway. For example, it enables a student to stop talking to his/her friends when the instructor begins class.

Dorsolateral Prefrontal Cortex

The dorsolateral prefrontal cortex helps direct attention appropriately, so tasks and class assignments are completed in an organized and efficient manner (Peterson & Welsh, 2014). This area of the brain also prevents the problem of over-focusing on one aspect of a task or situation. The dorsolateral prefrontal cortex also plays a role in social interactions by directing attention to social cues in conversations and by facilitating communication and problem solving.

Hippocampus

The hippocampus facilitates learning from past experiences and helps with the anticipation of future events (Zeithamova et al., 2012). For example, a student may have learned strategies that enable them to finish a test quickly and answer questions correctly because of his/her previous experience in taking similar types of exams.

Parietal Lobe

The parietal lobe is essential for keeping track of time. Importantly, it allows for the accurate estimation of how much time a given task is going to take (Battelli et al., 2007). This region of the brain also allows for the planning and completion of tasks, such as long-term course assignments.

Prefrontal Cortex

The prefrontal cortex systematically puts together all information from other brain areas to allow for informed decision making (Goldstein et al., 2014). In other words, the prefrontal cortex acts as a conductor and orchestrates all executive functions. This region of the brain allows for safe, responsible decision making by weighing the consequences of decisions before they are made. This ability to think through the possible outcomes of any given course of action is the main tenet of problem solving. The prefrontal cortex also links together memories of past experiences, allowing for the recall of outcomes from prior decisions so this information can be used to inform problem solving in the present. For example, a student who failed an exam because he/she decided to wait until the night before to study, may recall this experience and choose a different course of action (e.g., studying each night of the week prior to the exam) when planning how to prepare for an upcoming exam.

Skill Introduction: Contingent Self-Rewards

Describe

Introduce the concept of contingent self-rewards and its important. Hard work should be rewarded, otherwise sustained motivation to complete difficult or uninteresting tasks is unlikely. If completing a task does not automatically produce feelings of accomplishment (i.e., internally rewarding), then an external reward should be identified and given immediately following the completion of the task.

Demonstrate

Provide examples of how to set goals and pair them with rewards to increase the likelihood of task completion. Oftentimes, larger goals need to be broken down into smaller goals, and rewards that are motivating should be paired with completion of each smaller goal and the larger goal. The size of the reward should be dependent upon the amount of effort or time put into achieving the goal. An example of making use of this skill would be setting a running schedule to prepare for a half marathon (i.e., larger goal) and having a relaxing soak in a hot tub as a reward at the end of each run (e.g., smaller goals).

Discuss

Ask group members to come up with one or two examples of a larger goal that can be broken up into smaller goals. Have group members assign rewards to each smaller goal that are reinforcing to them. Provide group members with the opportunity to ask questions about the use of contingent self-rewards. Encourage groups members to reward themselves for attending the group session.

Wrap-Up

- ◆ Allow for questions: Ask group members if they have any questions about the purpose, expectations, or structure of the GOALS program; the role of executive functions; and the benefits of contingent self-rewards.
- ◆ Session review: Group leaders should briefly review the topics covered during this session.
    - • Expectations for both group leaders and group members

- Structure of group sessions and how skills are taught
- Importance of executive functions and how they impact functioning
- Brief introduction to using self-rewards to maintain motivation

♦ Distribute Appendix 1.1: Session 1 Outline and Appendix 1.3: Self-Rewards & Barriers to Success (Homework)

♦ Assign homework
  - Instruct group members to make a list of five to ten rewards that will motivate them to complete tasks they tend to avoid but must be completed (e.g., mentally taxing course assignments).
  - Group members should identify a class in which they would like to improve their performance and write down three to five barriers that may be impeding their success in that class.
  - Have group members print or download a syllabus from a current course and bring it to the next session.

♦ **Closing thoughts**—Highlight the following points:
  - Group members will be making changes to their routines based on the skills they learn in the program. These changes may feel strange at first. Group members may feel as if they need to force themselves to make changes, or they may feel nervous that they are not doing things correctly. These feelings are expected and normal. Encourage group members by acknowledging that the more these skills are practiced, the more natural using these skills will become.
  - While group leaders provide guidance regarding how to apply newly learned skills, group members are ultimately responsible for applying and practicing these skills in real-life situations. Practicing these skills outside of group meetings is essential to skill internalization (i.e., skills are used automatically and accurately), and homework is an important part of skill practice.
  - Encourage group members to openly communicate with group leaders by asking questions or raising any concerns they may have.

♦ Remind group members of the next session time, place, and topics to be covered:
  - Session 2: Self-Advocacy and Building Motivation
  - Group members will learn how to locate campus resources and effectively communicate with course instructors to address any problems they may be having in class. They will be taught how to extract important information from their course syllabi so important course deadlines are not missed. Finally, group members will learn how to properly use self-rewards to build and maintain their motivation to complete various tasks.

Table 1.1 Session 1 Fidelity Checklist

Task	Rating		
	0	1	2
Prepared materials for the session (i.e., printed handouts for all group members and provided binders)			
Provided an overview of the GOALS Program including: ♦ Overall objectives			

(Continued)

Table 1.1 (Continued)

Task	Rating		
	0	1	2
♦ Summary of content covered in each session (1–10) ♦ Expectations for group members while participating in the program ♦ GOALS teaching method (describe, demonstrate, and discuss)			
Provided psychoeducation regarding the importance of executive functions			
Described contingent self-rewards and demonstrated their use by providing examples of goals paired with appropriate rewards			
Asked questions to assess group members' understanding of contingent self-rewards and to promote engagement			
Assigned homework based on topic covered during this session			
Offered opportunity for group members to ask questions about the current session			
Mentioned date and topic of the next session			

0—Group Leader did not execute task.
1—Group Leader partially executed task.
2—Group Leader fully executed task.

References

Battelli, L., Pascual-Leone, A., & Cavanagh, P. (2007). The 'when' pathway of the right parietal lobe. *Trends in Cognitive Sciences, 11*(5), 204–210. 10.1016/j.tics.2007.03.001

Goldstein, S., Naglieri, J.A., Princiotta, D., & Otero, T.M. (2014). Introduction: A history of executive functioning as a theoretical and clinical construct. In S. Goldstein & J.A. Naglieri (Eds.), *Handbook of executive functioning* (pp. 3–11). Springer. 10.1007/978-1-4614-8106-5

Hooker, C.I., & Knight, R.T. (2006). The role of lateral orbitofrontal cortex in the inhibitory control of emotion. In D. Zald & S. Rauch (Eds.), *The Orbitofrontal Cortex.* (pp. 307–324). Oxford University Press. 10.1093/acprof:oso/9780198565741.001.0001

Peterson, E., & Welsh, M.C. (2014). The development of hot and cool executive functions in childhood and adolescence: Are we getting warmer? In S. Goldstein & J.A. Naglieri (Eds.), *Handbook of executive functioning* (pp. 45–65). Springer. 10.1007/978-1-4614-8106-5

Zeithamova, D., Schlichting, M.L., & Preston, A.R. (2012). The hippocampus and inferential reasoning: Building memories to navigate future decisions. *Frontiers in Human Neuroscience, 6*, 1–14. 10.3389/fnhum.2012.00070

Appendix 1.1: Session 1 Outline

Introduction to the Group for Organization, Attention and Learning Skills (GOALS)

- ♦ **Program objectives**
  - Plan and prioritize your daily tasks
  - Take notes and study more effectively
  - Cope with stressful situations and learn to control strong emotions
  - Access campus resources that may help facilitate academic success
  - Become your own self-advocate by communicating more effectively
  - Gain and maintain motivation toward achieving your goals
- ♦ **Expectations and obligations**
  - *Electronics:* Cell phones, laptops, tablets, and other electronic devices must be turned off and put away during group.
  - *Participation:* Respectful participation by all group members is essential. Respectful participation means listening to the input of other group members without judgement and contributing to the discussion by asking relevant questions or elaborating upon (e.g., providing examples) content covered in the session.
  - *Attendance:* It is important that you attend a MINIMUM of eight out of ten sessions. In other words, you are allowed to miss no more than three sessions during the course of the program. If you must miss a group meeting, contact group leaders at least 24 hours in advance to let them know you will be absent.
  - *Punctuality:* Be on time for group. This is very important because there is a lot of material to cover and you need to be present to learn it. Because sessions are time-limited, group leaders will not be able to go back over topics introduced earlier in the session for the benefit of those who are late to group.
  - *Confidentiality:* Confidentiality is of the utmost importance. Private information shared in group should never be discussed outside of group sessions.
  - *Preparedness:* You are expected to complete the homework assignments given to you each week. Homework is important as it allows you to practice the skills you learn in group and apply them in real-world situations. Finishing your homework before coming to session also gives you the opportunity to problem-solve challenges with group leaders' help.
- ♦ **Basic program schedule**
  - Session 1: Introduction to the GOALS Program
  - Session 2: Self-Advocacy and Building Motivation
  - Session 3: Taking Notes from Lectures and Course Readings
  - Session 4: Time Awareness and Tuning Out Distractions
  - Session 5: Prioritizing and Scheduling Tasks
  - Session 6: Program Review and Getting Organized

- Session 7: Overcoming Procrastination and Coping with Stress
- Session 8: Planning a Long-Term Project
- Session 9: Studying for Tests of Varying Formats
- Session 10: Summary of Program and Progress Made

♦ **Executive functions**

EFs are higher-order cognitive or mental processes (e.g., attentional control, working memory, planning, flexible thinking, and the ability to regulate behaviors and emotions) that underlie goal-directed behavior and are orchestrated by the prefrontal cortex in the brain. EFs are essential for success in all areas of life (i.e., academic, occupational, and social). Refer to Executive Functions Psychoeducation Handout for review.

♦ **Contingent self-rewards**

To increase and sustain your motivation, your hard work should be rewarded! If you do not automatically feel a sense of accomplishment (i.e., internal reward) when completing a task, give yourself an external reward as soon as you complete the task. Remember:

- Larger goals often need to be broken down into smaller goals. Give yourself small rewards for the completion of each small goal, and pair a large reward with the completion of the overarching or larger goal.
- The size of the reward should match the amount of effort or time put into achieving your goal.
- **Example:** When setting up a study schedule for an upcoming exam, completion of each study session would serve as your smaller goals, and taking the exam would serve as your overarching or larger goal. If you find walks around campus enjoyable, you may decide to study for 50 minutes each evening for the 2 weeks leading up to an exam and reward yourself with a ten to fifteen-minute walk after each study session. Once you have taken the exam, you would give yourself a larger reward such as going to a movie with friends.

Appendix 1.2: Session 1 Handout

Executive Functions Psychoeducation

Orbitofrontal Cortex

The orbitofrontal cortex helps control behaviors by inhibiting reactions to strong urges or feelings. For example, it prevents you from hitting someone when you are angry or blurting out random thoughts during a class lecture. The orbitofrontal cortex also helps stop behaviors that are already underway. For example, it enables you to stop talking to your friends when the instructor begins class.

Dorsolateral Prefrontal Cortex

The dorsolateral prefrontal cortex helps direct your attention appropriately, so tasks and class assignments are completed in an organized and efficient manner. Importantly, this area of the brain prevents you from getting over-focused on one aspect of a task or situation. The dorsolateral prefrontal cortex also plays a role in social interactions by directing your attention to social cues in conversations and by facilitating communication and problem solving.

Hippocampus

The hippocampus allows you to learn from past experiences and helps you anticipate future events. For example, a student may have learned strategies that enable them to finish a test quickly and answer questions correctly because of their previous experience in taking similar types of exams.

Parietal Lobe

The parietal lobe allows you to keep track of time so you can accurately estimate how much time is required for a given activity. This region of the brain also allows for the planning and completion of activities, such as long-term course assignments.

Prefrontal Cortex

The prefrontal cortex systematically puts together all information from other brain areas to allow for informed decision making. Simply stated, it orchestrates all executive functions. This region of the brain helps you make safe, responsible decisions by enabling you to weigh the consequences of your decisions before making them. The prefrontal cortex also links you to memories of past experiences, allowing you to recall the outcomes of prior decisions and to use this information to inform problem solving in the present. For example, if you failed an exam because you decided to wait until the night before to study, you may recall this experience and choose a different course of action (e.g., studying each night of the week prior to the exam) when planning how to prepare for an upcoming exam.

Appendix 1.3: Session 1 Homework

Self-Rewards and Barriers to Success

1. Reward yourself for attending this session – it is important that this reward matches the amount of effort you made during group. Record your reward in the space provided below.

2. Make a list of five to ten rewards that are reinforcing to you and will motivate you to complete tasks that you tend to avoid, but must be completed (e.g., mentally taxing course assignments).

   1.
   2.
   3.
   4.
   5.
   6.
   7.
   8.
   9.
   10.

3. Identify a class in which you would like to improve your performance. Write down three to five barriers that may be getting in the way of you reaching your full potential.

   Class: _____
   1.
   2.
   3.
   4.
   5.

Chapter 2

Self-Advocacy and Building Motivation

Quick Look

Objectives

- Learn how to extract important information from course syllabi.
- Discover how to locate on-campus resources vital for student success.
- Understand how to effectively communicate with instructors and administrators, including how to have productive conversations with instructors so that they are better equipped to perform well in their courses.
- Be introduced to the concept of self-rewards and how to implement this skill.
- Develop a list of contingent self-rewards that may be used throughout the semester to motivate and reward goal setting and attainment.

Materials Needed

- Appendix 2.1: Session 2 Outline
- Appendix 2.2: Extracting Vital Information from a Course Syllabus (Handout)
- Appendix 2.3: Instructor Role-Plays (Activity)
- Appendix 2.4: Campus Resources Handout Development Guide and Template
- Note: This guide is designed to help group leaders develop a handout that contains information about the types of on-campus resources available to group members. An alternative is to obtain an equivalent handout that has already been developed by the University. An optional fill-in-the-blank Campus Resources Handout template is provided.
- Appendix 2.5: Accessing Accommodations (Handout)
- Appendix 2.6: Emailing an Instructor (Handout)
- Appendix 2.7: Effective Communication Worksheet (Homework)
- Appendix 2.8: Self-Rewards List (Homework)
- Appendix 2.9: Self-Rewards Implementation Worksheet (Homework)
- *Optional:* Session 2 Fidelity Checklist (Table 2.1)

DOI: 10.4324/9781003199618-3

Session Highlights

- ◆ Check-in
  - • Discuss content covered in the previous session (Introduction to the GOALS Program)
  - • Review Session 1 homework (Self-Rewards and Barriers to Success)
- ◆ Learn new skills
  - • Extract important information from course syllabi
  - • Effective communication and locating on-campus student resources
  - • Self-rewards
- ◆ Wrap-up
  - • Assign homework
  - • Discuss content of the upcoming session

Detailed Session Content

Check-In

- ◆ Briefly review topics covered last week.
  - • Ask group members to summarize Session 1
  - • Material covered during the last session:
    - □ Group structure and expectations
    - □ Psychoeducation on executive functions
    - □ Brief introduction to self-rewards
  - • Answer any questions about the material covered during the previous session
- ◆ Homework review
  - • Ask group members to share the self-rewards they used for attending Session 1.
    - □ If necessary, discuss any barriers that prevented them from using self-rewards and formulate a plan for homework completion. For example, if group members explain that they forgot to do the homework, ask them where they could place a reminder note or the homework sheet to prompt them to do the assignment.
  - • Have group members refer to the Self-Rewards and Barriers to Success Homework Handout and instruct them to give examples of barriers that they identified on this handout as interfering with their academic success.

Tip for Group Leaders: Make sure to write down these barriers as they are asked to refer to them when discussing effective communication and on-campus resources.

Skills Introduction: Extracting Important Information From Course Syallabi

Describe

An important initial step that can be taken to increase the chances of performing well in each course is to carefully read the course syllabus before (if it is available) or immediately after the initial class meeting. The syllabus is a contract between the student and instructor so it should be continually referred to throughout the semester to ensure important dates are not missed (e.g., assignment due dates and unit exams). It also allows students to assess whether the course meets their educational goals, which is something to consider given the time commitment needed to meet all course requirements.

Demonstrate

Have group members take out the course syllabus that they were asked to bring to session and distribute Appendix 2.2: Extracting Vital Information from a Course Syllabus (Handout). Review the handout and encourage group members to isolate relevant information by underlining or highlighting it. If time permits, assist group members in adding important course dates to their planners or calendars.

Skills Introduction: Effective Communication and On-Campus Resources

Describe

Effective communication with instructors is essential if students wish to have their needs met and to obtain tips for success across courses of varying formats. This skill must be regularly and intentionally practiced so that these conversations are productive and goal-oriented when the time comes to act as a self-advocate. Here are some general tips to consider when communicating with an instructor in person, remotely, or in written form:

♦ **Address the instructor respectfully and always use his/her proper title.** Your instructor's title may be listed on the course syllabus. Address the instructor as Dr. "last name" if he/she has a doctoral degree. If unsure of the instructor's title, err on the side of caution and address the instructor as Dr. "last name." If the instructor does not have a doctoral degree, he/she will correct the mistake and will likely not be offended.

♦ **Visit the instructor during their office hours or schedule a meeting.** Instructors are often required to set aside regular office hours each week. However, it may be helpful to set up an individual meeting to give the instructor time to prepare and ensure there is sufficient time to discuss any problems and solutions to those problems.

♦ **Be polite and respectful.** Make requests (e.g., "I would like to meet with you"), NOT demands (e.g., "You need to meet with me tomorrow") when communicating with instructors.

♦ **Express appreciation.** When meeting with an instructor, express gratitude for the instructor's time and assistance.

♦ **Be honest.** Instructors need to know exactly what is going on so they can effectively help. It is counterproductive to make up excuses, minimize, or lie about problems.

♦ **Talk with instructors about perceived problems as early as possible.** If issues are recognized and addressed promptly, it will be easier to overcome them. Do not wait until the last minute (e.g., the day before the exam) to seek help.

If struggling in a particular course (e.g., not receiving a passing grade on the first exam or assignment), it is a good idea to reach out to that instructor to set up a meeting so that problems may be addressed immediately, and a plan is devised of how to better prepare for graded coursework. The following steps outline how to set up a meeting with an instructor and how to communicate in a way that will maximize time spent with that instructor:

♦ **Email the instructor** to set up a meeting or **determine** the instructor's office hours by referring to the course syllabus. (Refer to Appendix 2.6: Emailing an Instructor Handout.)

♦ **Prepare specific problems to be discussed and addressed.** The more specific the description of the problem is, the better an instructor will be able to help address it. Potential points for discussion include:
  • Trouble understanding the material
  • Performing poorly on tests despite knowing and understanding the material
  • Difficulty keeping up with the pace of the lecture and taking helpful notes

♦ **Ask the instructor for suggestions on effective strategies for success in his/her class.** Instructors can often provide useful tips on ways to approach the material covered and how to complete assignments required in their classes.

♦ **Take notes** during meetings with instructors rather than relying on memory to recall the suggestions that instructors made. Taking notes will provide a good foundation for a plan of action.

♦ **Follow through on what is learned**. For the instructor's suggestions to be helpful, it is necessary that they are incorporated into weekly course preparation and study routines. For example, if an instructor recommends that a student supplement his/her lecture notes with notes taken from course readings, the student should set aside and schedule additional time to take notes from these readings while cross-referencing this information with the notes taken during class. If additional questions or concerns come up, it is important to follow up with the instructor.

Demonstrate

♦ Group leaders are to act out both the Ineffective Communication and Effective Communication Role Plays (Appendix 2.3) in front of group members. After each role play, ask group members to provide feedback on what aspects of the role play were effective and what aspects were ineffective.

♦ Divide students into pairs to practice approaching an instructor about an upcoming writing assignment or test. Make sure to quickly review the steps outlined above on how to appropriately approach and ask an instructor for help.

Discuss

♦ Ask group members which strategies were the most effective during the role play practice. The following questions may be used to prompt further discussion:
  • What may get in the way of group members using these strategies when communicating with instructors?
  • What can be done to ensure that group members follow through with the suggestions offered by their instructors?

♦ Re-emphasize that meeting with an instructor is only the first step. Group members need to use what is learned in these meetings and apply it to their course preparation and study routines to be successful.

♦ Inform group members that course instructors are one resource they may use if struggling academically; however, there are other on-campus resources available to them. Distribute both the Campus Resources Handout (Appendix 2.4) compiled by group leaders and the Accessing Accommodations handout (Appendix 2.5). Briefly highlight what services are offered to students. Group leaders may offer to set up individual meeting times with any group members seeking further guidance regarding these resources. Keep in mind that this may be a group member's first time independently seeking out resources and advocating for services.

Skills Introduction: Self-Rewards

Describe

Extrinsic rewards are rewards that are allocated after completing a task or reaching a goal and are external to a person. Examples include money or a good grade. ***Intrinsic rewards*** give personal satisfaction, so they are internal to a person. Intrinsic rewards may include a sense of pride, feelings of accomplishment, or an impression that time has been spent contributing to a meaningful goal. An example of an activity that might be intrinsically rewarding would be volunteering at a career center to identify ways to strengthen a resume for those seeking employment. The ultimate goal is to increase both intrinsic and extrinsic rewards to maximize motivation to initiate and complete tasks that would otherwise not be necessarily enjoyable.

Contingent self-rewards are activities that are typically low cost but increase motivation to follow-through on a task. Contingent self-rewards should be proportional to the amount of effort expended to complete the activity (e.g., study for one hour and take a ten-minute break). Larger tasks may be broken down into smaller tasks that are subsequently rewarded after their completion. For example, test preparation may be broken down into smaller increments and after each study period is completed a reward is given. Rewards may be classified as "mini-motivators," small rewards, medium rewards, and large rewards and should correspond with the amount of time each reward takes. A word of caution—small rewards can easily turn into medium rewards if too much time is spent engaging in the reward (e.g., watching TV or chatting with friends). It is important that the reward chosen is motivating enough to stay on-task and does not become counterproductive by diverting attention away from the activity that needs to be completed. A good rule of thumb is that for every 50 minutes spent on coursework or another task, 10 minutes should be reserved for a reward. A stopwatch is an ideal way to monitor the time it takes to complete a task and the time it takes to engage in a reward.

Demonstrate

♦ Provide an example of how to make use of contingent self-rewards. The following example may be used to illustrate how contingent self-rewards may be put into practice.

• A student decides to begin preparing for a statistics test a week in advance by building in motivators to learn the material. Each evening, the student studies for an hour, then rewards himself/herself by walking his/her dog or having a snack (10 to 15-minute break). After studying for a total of three hours, the student rewards himself/herself by watching an episode of his/her favorite TV show. After the test is over, the student rewards by going out with friends.

♦ Ask group members to share tasks for which they lack motivation to complete.

• Write down examples of tasks solicited from group members, then ask for appropriate, contingent self-rewards that could be paired with these tasks.

Discuss

♦ Assess group members' understanding of how to use contingent self-rewards by revisiting the list of rewards they completed for Session 1 homework (Self-Rewards and Barriers to Success; Appendix 1.3). The following questions may be used to promote further discussion:

• What rewards on group members' self-rewards lists are mini-motivators, small rewards, medium rewards, and large rewards?

• Are there additional rewards group members could add to their lists?

• Are there any unique rewards group members would like to share with the group?

• Would contingent self-rewards be extrinsically or intrinsically motivating?

- What might get in the way of using self-rewards? How could group members address these obstacles?

Wrap-Up

♦ Allow for questions: Give group members an opportunity to ask questions about this session's material.
♦ Session review: Group leaders should briefly review the topics covered during the current session.
  - Extracting relevant information from course syllabi
  - Effective communication with instructors
  - Accessing on-campus resources
  - Contingent self-rewards
♦ Distribute Session 2 outline (Appendix 2.1), Effective Communication Worksheet (Appendix 2.7), Self-Rewards List (Appendix 2.8), and Self-Rewards Implementation Worksheet (Appendix 2.9).
♦ Assign homework
  - Effective Communication Worksheet (Appendix 2.7): Group members are to contact an instructor for a class in which they are currently having difficulties. Following this meeting, group members are to complete this worksheet to document how the meeting went (e.g., feedback given by the instructor and actions taken by the group member to act on feedback).
  - Self-Rewards List (Appendix 2.8): Group members are to add rewards to each category on the Self-Rewards List (Table 2.2) (i.e., mini motivators, small rewards, medium rewards, and large rewards). Examples of rewards that fit into each category are provided on the worksheet, and group members are free to use any of these rewards on their own list. Explain to group members that they should list more mini motivators and small rewards than medium and large rewards given most tasks they list will take less than 60 minutes to complete.
  - Self-Rewards Implementation Worksheet (Appendix 2.9): Group members are to record tasks they need to complete in the upcoming week, and then document what rewards they gave themselves for completing each task. Group members should also record any issues they encountered when using self-rewards and any strategies they used to ensure follow-through with using this skill.
♦ Remind group members of the next session time, place, and topics to be covered.
  - Session 3: Taking notes from lectures and course readings
♦ Group members will understand how to take thorough and helpful notes during class lectures, reading assignments, and other class-related activities.

Table 2.1 Session 2 Fidelity Checklist

Task	Rating		
	0	**1**	**2**
Prepared materials for the session (i.e., prepared campus resources handout prior to session and printed handouts for all group members)			
Reviewed topics covered at previous session			
Discussed homework assignment from previous session			
Offered opportunity for group members to ask questions about the previous session			
Asked each group member to identify and extract information from their course syllabi			
Demonstrated both communication role-plays (i.e., effective and ineffective) and solicited feedback			
Divided group members into pairs to practice effective communication			
Demonstrated contingent self-reward use by providing examples to group members			
Solicited examples of tasks for which group members lack motivation and appropriate self-rewards that could be paired with those tasks.			
Assessed group members' understanding of contingent self-reward use by revisiting the list of rewards they completed for Session 1 homework			
Asked questions to assess group members understanding of the skills and to promote engagement			
Offered opportunity for group members to ask questions about the current session			
Assigned homework based on topics covered during this session			
Mentioned date and topic of the next session			

0—Group Leader did not execute task.
1—Group Leader partially executed task.
2—Group Leader fully executed task.

Appendix 2.1: Session 2 Outline

Self-Advocacy and Building Motivation

SKILL: Extracting Important Information From Course Syllabi

- ♦ Reviewing the syllabus for each of your courses is a great way to increase your chances of academic success.
- ♦ A syllabus provides much of the information needed to successfully complete a course.
- ♦ Review the course syllabus before (if it is available) or immediately after the initial class meeting, refer to it throughout the course, and update the syllabus as well as their planners or calendars with any changes made by the instructor.

SKILL: Effective Communication

General Tips

- ♦ **Address your instructor respectfully and always use his/her proper title.** Your instructor's title may be listed on the course syllabus. Address your instructor as Dr. "last name" if they have a doctoral degree, and err on the side of caution by addressing your instructor as Dr. "last name" if you are unsure of their title. If your instructor does not have a doctoral degree, he/she may correct you but won't be offended.
- ♦ **Either visit your instructor during their office hours or schedule a meeting (see Emailing Your Instructors handout).** Instructors are often required to set aside regular office hours each week. However, it may be helpful to set up an individual meeting to give the instructor time to prepare and ensure you have sufficient time to discuss any problems and their solutions.
- ♦ **Be polite and respectful.** Be sure that you don't sound demanding when communicating with your instructor. Make requests (e.g., "I would like to meet with you"), NOT demands ("You need to meet with me tomorrow").
- ♦ **Express appreciation.** When you meet with an instructor, you should express gratitude for their time and assistance.
- ♦ **Be Honest.** Your instructor needs to know exactly what is going on to effectively help you. Do not make excuses, minimize your problems, or lie about the problems you are having.
- ♦ **Talk with your instructors about perceived problems as *early* as possible.** If you recognize and address issues early, you will have an easier time overcoming them. Do not wait until the last minute (e.g., the day before an exam) to seek help.

Scheduling and Preparing for Your Meeting

- ♦ **Reach out to your instructor.** Email your instructor (see Emailing an Instructor Handout for guidance) to set up a meeting ordetermine the instructor's office hours by referring to the course syllabus.

- ♦ **Prepare specific problems to be discussed and addressed.** The more specific you can be in describing your problem, the better your instructor will be able to help you. Do you have trouble understanding the material? Do you understand the material, but you just don't do well on tests? Do you have trouble keeping up with the pace of the lecture and taking the appropriate notes?
  - Prepare a list of these topics and concerns to bring to the meeting.
- ♦ **Ask your instructor for suggestions on effective strategies for success in their class.** Instructors can often provide very useful tips on effective ways to approach the material covered and how to complete the assignments required in their classes.
- ♦ **Take notes.** You should always take notes during meetings with your instructors rather than rely on your memory to recall the suggestions that your instructors made. Taking notes will help you to walk away from your meeting with a good foundation for a plan of action.

Following Through on What You Learn During Your Meeting

- ♦ Apply what you learn in your meeting to achieve success in the course. It is necessary to incorporate your instructor's suggestions into your weekly class preparation and study routines.
- ♦ Follow up with your instructor if you have any additional questions or concerns (e.g., review performance on a test and ask about a difficult concept).

Skill: Self-Rewards

- ♦ **Extrinsic rewards:** Rewards that are allocated after completing a task or reaching a goal and are externally motivating (e.g., earning a paycheck).
- ♦ **Intrinsic rewards:** Give personal satisfaction, so that they are internally motivating (e.g., volunteering at a homeless shelter).
- ♦ **Goal:** Increase both intrinsic and extrinsic rewards so that you are both internally and externally motivated to reach your personal goals.
  - Self-rewards may be used to help you elicit motivation to initiate and complete tasks that you do not necessarily enjoy.
  - Contingent self-rewards are primarily **extrinsic**.
- ♦ **Contingent self-rewards:** Activities that are typically low cost, but will increase your motivation to follow-through on a task
  - "Contingent" = *proportional* to the difficulty of the activity you completed (e.g., ten-minute break after studying for one hour)
  - Larger tasks may be broken down into smaller tasks that are rewarded after their completion (e.g., break test prep into smaller increments and give yourself a reward after each study period is completed).
  - Rewards can be classified as mini-motivators, small rewards, medium rewards, and large rewards.
- ♦ **Remember:** It is easy for small rewards to turn into medium rewards if you spend too much time watching TV or chatting with friends.
  - Rule of thumb: For every 50 minutes you spend on a school assignment or task, ten minutes should be reserved for a reward.

- Important that the reward you engage in keeps you on-task for the activity you want to complete.
- Use a stopwatch to closely monitor the time you take to complete a task and the time you take to engage in a reward.

Appendix 2.2: Session 2 Handout

Extracting Vital Information From a Course Syllabus

What is a course syllabus?

A course syllabus provides the framework for a course and offers a recipe for the success of students. At the most basic level, a syllabus informs students what the course is about, where and when it is held, who is teaching it, and what is required to pass. Additionally, instructors may add information about class etiquette and expectations, rubrics for assignments, and other helpful resources. While each academic institution has its own requirements for what must be included in a syllabus, there are some elements that will always be included and are helpful for students.

Important Elements of a Syllabus

Course Information

At a minimum, the syllabus will include the title of the course, a description of the course, and learning objectives. The location, time, and days of class meetings will also be included. Often, prerequisites or courses that are required to be taken before enrolling in the course are listed.

From this section, it is important that you note when and where the course will be held and add it to your planner or calendar. Note if there are laboratory-based or online components to the course, which may necessitate additional meeting times, and be sure to include this information in your calendar or planner. It is also a good idea to verify that you have completed all pre-requisites for the course. Finally, the course description and learning objectives may be helpful in determining whether you wish to take the course and if it aligns with your academic or career goals.

Instructor Information

The syllabus will include the name of the instructor, as well as their contact information (email, phone number, office location, etc.). The name of the teaching assistant for the course may also be included, if applicable. Other information in the syllabus includes when and where office hours are held and the instructor's preferred method of contact.

As discussed in Session 2, pay close attention to the title of the instructor so you know how to address them and add the instructor's office hours in your planner or calendar.

Required Materials

If applicable, the syllabus will include what textbook is required for the course, as well as citations of other reading materials. These additional readings and other supplementary materials are often provided electronically by the instructor or they are available through the university library—make sure to verify where these materials can be found if it is not clear in the syllabus.

Finally, the technology and software used in the course (e.g., Canvas and Blackboard) or needed by the student (e.g., Adobe Reader and Microsoft Office) will be specified.

Be sure to note what materials are required and gain access to them as quickly as possible. In particular, it is important to have the required textbook in your possession prior to the first day of class so you do not fall behind with the required readings.

Assignments and Evaluations

The syllabus will include a list of all assignments or other methods of evaluation used by the instructor, such as projects, papers, quizzes, or exams, as well as the maximum value of points or weights (% of grade) assigned to each one. Typically, the syllabus will also include a detailed description of these assignments. This section of the syllabus is **EXTREMELY** important, as it outlines how your grade for the course will be calculated. Pay close attention to several important aspects of these methods of evaluation, such as whether or not exams are cumulative, how to format assignments, or if rubrics (i.e., grading criteria for an assignment) are provided.

Due dates for assignments and exams should be added to your planner or calendar as soon as you receive the syllabus. It may be helpful to add reminders for these events a few days or weeks prior to their due dates so you can plan accordingly.

Course Outline/Schedule

The core of the syllabus includes a schedule of topics covered during each class meeting and relevant readings or assignments that are to be completed for that class. This information may be presented in a variety of ways, but is often in tabular format (i.e., rows and columns). The expected due dates for assignments, exam dates, as well as scheduled holidays and breaks are also listed in the course schedule.

The course schedule is arguably the most important section of the syllabus! Ideally, all dates outlined on the course syllabus should be entered into your planner or calendar. It may feel daunting to do this all at once, so upcoming dates may be added on the first day of each month or at designated times throughout the semester. Regardless, it is recommended that you consult the course schedule regularly to ensure that all required tasks are completed on time.

Policies and Procedures

Oftentimes, this section will be more generic compared to other sections of the syllabus. There are specific policies in place mandated by the University that instructors are required to include in their syllabus. Such policies may outline expectations and procedures for attendance, academic integrity (e.g., plagiarism and cheating), withdrawing/dropping of a course, and disability accommodations. However, it is still important to review this section, as some instructors may include course-specific policies that may impact your participation.

Keep in Mind

Every syllabus is subject to change. Although such changes may be frustrating, it is impossible for instructors to predict everything that will happen during a semester. As such, note any changes and update them accordingly in your planner or calendar. Also, **ALWAYS** consult your syllabus before you ask the instructor about an assignment, due date, or class policy. Your instructor spent a great deal of time and effort to develop the syllabus for your benefit, and most questions can be answered by simply reviewing it.

Appendix 2.3: Session 2 Activity

Instructor Role-Plays

Role-Play 1: Ineffective Communication

Student: *(Student does not have notebook or pen)* Hi _____! *(Student greets instructor by his or her first name).* I wanted to talk about some problems I'm having with class during our meeting.

Instructor: Hi _____, come on in. What are you struggling with?

Student: Well, I didn't do well on the last exam, and we have another one coming up next Monday. So, I was wondering what questions will be on it.

Instructor: I don't tell students what specific questions will be on exams. You should study the material discussed in class and the information presented in assigned readings for this unit. To help students identify what material they should focus on, I post my lecture slides to the course website before every class.

Student: I don't understand the material at all.

Instructor: What are some of the specific questions that you have?

Student: I'm not sure. I was hoping that you could go over the material for the second exam with me. I'm just not getting it.

Instructor: Well, it is a lot of material and it would be difficult to re-teach all of it during this meeting. If you study your notes, review my slides, and come up with some questions about things that you are struggling with, I would be happy to discuss those topics with you. I have office hours from 1–3 in the afternoon on Thursday and Friday. You are more than welcome to come back with some more specific questions then.

Student: Okay, have a nice afternoon _____. I'll drop by in a few days.

Role-Play 2: Effective Communication

Student: *(Has Pen and Notebook in Hand)* Hi Dr. _____! My name is _____ and I'm the student from your History 101 class that emailed you about meeting today. Thank you for seeing me.

Instructor: Hi _____! Come on in and have a seat. How can I help you today?

(Continued)

Student:	I seem to be struggling with preparing for the class exams. I didn't do very well on the first exam we took last week, even though I felt like I understood the material during your lectures.
Instructor:	How did you prepare for the exam?
Student:	I studied the lecture slides that you provided on the course website for a few hours each afternoon for three days before the exam.
Instructor:	I would suggest that you break the material into more manageable sections, instead of trying to learn it all in a short period of time.
Student:	Do you have any suggestions on effective ways to organize the material for studying?
Instructor:	This material can be challenging, and if you study small sections every week instead of waiting until the week of the exam, you will probably have a much easier time learning the material and remembering it on exam day.
Student:	So, studying the material in smaller sections is definitely something I can work on, but I'm not really sure how to study the material so the information stays with me. For the first exam, I studied by reading your lecture slides several times.
Instructor:	One strategy that past students have found helpful, is to take each week's lecture and create flashcards with the notes written in your own words. By working through the material and converting it into your own words, you will develop a deeper understanding of the information. You will essentially be learning as you prepare to study, and while studying the flash cards themselves.
Student:	(*taking notes while instructor is talking*)
Student:	That suggestion sounds like it will be very helpful. Thank you. (*Refers to Paper*) Do you have any other general suggestions on how to do well in your class?
Instructor:	Other than studying the exam material as it is given to you, I would suggest that you form a study group with some of your fellow students—sometimes going over class material in groups can be very helpful. Other students may see the material in a different way that will help you understand difficult topics, and it will give you an opportunity to teach the material to other students which tends to foster a deeper understanding of the information.
Student:	If I follow all of these suggestions we talked about, but I still feel like I am struggling with some of the material what do you recommend that I do?
Instructor:	If you recognize issues early, you will have a much easier time addressing them. Either make an appointment or come by during my office hours if you feel like you are having problems with any of the material. Be sure to identify material that is challenging to you and have your questions prepared before our meeting, so I can be more deliberate in my efforts to help you and we make the most of our time.
Student:	(*taking notes while instructor is talking*)
Student:	Thank you for all of these great suggestions. I can definitely take what we talked about and use it to do better in class. I really appreciate you taking the time to meet with me Dr. _____.
Instructor:	No problem! I'm always happy to meet with students and give advice.

Appendix 2.4

Campus Resources Handout Development Guide and Template

Group leaders can use the following information as a guide when building their group-specific handout. It is recommended that group leaders identify and provide helpful resources for both students' academic success and personal well-being. The demands of college can be extremely stressful and trying, so it is important to help students understand what help is available to them at the university and/or in the community.

Examples of the types of information that may be helpful to include in the Campus Resources handout are provided below.

Suggestions for group leaders to follow as they design each section of the handout are provided in the "Tip for Group Leaders" boxes. Any additional suggestions for group leaders that are included in section examples are italicized and bolded.

Academic Success

Tip for Group Leaders: Identify whether the college or university for which you are conducting GOALS has a program or center designed to increase student success. These types of university centers typically help new students transition into student life and support students' academic success through various programs. If the university does not have a central program that compiles student resources, group leaders should take the time to identify any relevant student support resources that are available and compile them along with their contact information in this section of the handout. Refer to the example below for an idea of how this information can be presented in your handout and the types of resources that may be helpful to group members.

Example Academic Success Section

Provide the website name and address as well as a description of the website and what makes it useful for students. Consider giving simple directions that students may follow to navigate any website you provide. Provide a brief list of important information the website maintains as well as any programs that may be helpful to student success.

- ♦ *Student Success at GOALS University*: [*Website link*]—Please take the time to browse through this webpage and become familiar with the resources available to you!
- ♦ By clicking on the "For Students" tab located on the left-hand side of the Student Success at GOALS University webpage, you can access links to many resources that have the potential to enhance your success and well-being! The following are just a few of the services available to GOALS University students:
  - Academic Help—This webpage is a compilation of tutoring and coaching services in various subjects including:
    - Academic coaching
      - Provides coaching in study skills, note taking, time management, and goal setting to assist with the transition to college demands.
    - Public speaking
      - Need help preparing for an upcoming class presentation? Having trouble organizing your speech? Feeling anxious? Schedule an appointment at the _____!
    - Writing tutoring
      - Having trouble with a writing project? Tutors at the _____ are ready to provide you with one-on-one instruction!
    - Math Tutoring
      - Need help in your basic math courses? Make an appointment at the _____ for one-on-one instruction.
    - Learning Center
      - Their services are designed to help you determine what type of learner you are and teach you strategies specifically designed for people with your individual learning styles.
    - Tutoring in specific subjects such as statistics, chemistry, biology, computing, foreign language, statistics, anthropology, construction, and Many More!!!

Personal Matters

Tip For Group Leaders: Include information regarding disability accommodations, mental health supports, and child care in this section of the Campus Resources handout.

- ♦ Most schools have an office that is responsible for coordinating services and accommodations for students with disabilities. Provide the name, contact information, and location for your school's appropriate office in this section of the handout.
- ♦ The transition to college can be an especially stressful life change, and it is important to include information identifying potentially helpful mental health supports that are available to students.
- ♦ Childcare can be very difficult to navigate as a new college student. Identify relevant childcare resources in the community and those affiliated with the school. Also, include any financial supports that may be available to students.

(Continued)

> Refer to the example below for an idea of the types of information and resources to include in this section of the handout.

Example Personal Matters Section

For any resource listed in this section, provide the name, location, and contact information (e.g., phone number, website, and/or relevant email addresses) as well as a brief description of services offered.

- ◆ *Disability Services Office*
  Located in GOALS Hall 111
  [Contact Information including phone number, email address, website]
  - Students who qualify may find it helpful to acquire testing accommodations through the DSO.
  - Exam and standardized test modifications include:
    - Extended test-taking time—Some individuals with disabilities may read at a slower rate, process information more slowly, and/or have more difficulty focusing than other students. For these individuals, extended test-taking time may be helpful.
    - A minimal distraction testing environment – Individuals with disabilities such as ADHD may have difficulty focusing and may be easily distracted by noises and movement in the classroom. Taking exams in a quiet and controlled environment may enhance the performance of students who struggle with tuning out these distractions.
- ◆ Community Counseling and Assessment
  - *The GOALS Psychology Clinic*
    - Located in Success Hall Room 214 *[phone number; website link]*
    - Clinicians provide high-quality assessment, therapy, and consultation services at a low cost. They provide therapeutic interventions for various psychological disorders, group services addressing specific needs or disorders, and learning disability/ADHD assessments to determine and recommend necessary accommodations.
  - *The Community Counseling and Assessment Clinic*
    - Located in Success Hall Room 213 *[phone number; website link]*
    - Counselors can help with personal, academic, and career issues. Counselors are available to help with emotional problems, listen to your ideas, help improve your academic skills, or provide support through a difficult transition.
  - *Counseling Services*
    - Located in Graduate Hall East *[phone number; website link]*
    - Counselors can help with anxiety, depression, family problems, motivation and time management, eating disorders, homesickness, and substance abuse.
- ◆ Childcare
  - Child Day Care Services & Early Childhood Education
    - Child Development Daycare Program – *[phone number; website]*: Their services are for children ages eight weeks to five years old, and are available to the general public.

The following fill-in-the-blank Campus Resources Handout template is provided as an option for group leaders. The form may be filled out by group leaders prior to the session and distributed to group members. Alternatively, group leaders may choose to develop their own handout or obtain an equivalent handout from their university or college.

Campus Resources

Academic Success

♦ **Helpful Websites**

• Website Link:	
Description:	
• Website Link:	
Description:	
• Website Link:	
Description:	

♦ **Services Available to Students** (e.g., academic coaching, public speaking, tutoring, etc.)

• Resource Name:	
Contact Information:	
Description of Services:	
• Resource Name:	

(*Continued*)

Contact Information:	
Description of Services:	
• Resource Name:	
Contact Information	
Description of Services:	
• Resource Name:	
Contact Information:	
Description of Services:	
• Resource Name:	
Contact Information:	
Description of Services:	
• Resource Name:	
Contact Information:	
Description of Services:	

Personal Matters

When college life feels overwhelming, there are services dedicated to helping you succeed: **Disability Accommodations**

• Office Name:	
Contact Information:	
Description of Services:	

♦ Community Counseling and Assessment

• Resource Name:	
Contact Information:	
Description of Services:	
• Resource Name:	
Contact Information:	
Description of Services:	
• Resource Name:	
Contact Information:	
Description of Services:	
• Resource Name:	
Contact Information:	
Description of Services:	

♦ Childcare and Financial Supports

• Resource Name:	
Contact Information:	
Description of Services:	
• Resource Name:	
Contact Information:	
Description of Services:	

(Continued)

• Resource Name:	
Contact Information:	
Description of Services:	
• Resource Name:	
Contact Information:	
Description of Services:	

Appendix 2.5: Session 2 Handout

Accessing Accommodations
The Americans With Disabilities Act (1990)

♦ **What is it?** The ADA is a civil rights law meant to protect people with disabilities from discrimination and to ensure that they have equal opportunities to participate in employment, purchase goods and services, and engage in government programs.

♦ **How does it protect students with disabilities?** Under the ADA, postsecondary institutions (i.e., colleges and universities) are required to provide the necessary accommodations when a student reports a disability and provides appropriate documentation of that disability (e.g., a comprehensive psychological report or documentation from a physician).

  • **Who has a disability?** Any person who "has a physical or mental impairment that substantially limits one or more major life activities"; "has a record of such an impairment" or is "regarded as having an impairment"

♦ **How do students access accommodations?** Postsecondary institutions typically have a disability services office (DSO) with which students work to develop and coordinate plans for the provision of reasonable accommodations that are specific to students' disabilities.

  • **Be proactive!** It's important to remember that schools can only provide accommodations once you have informed them of your disability and provided any necessary documentation.
    □ *It is the student's responsibility to initiate the accommodation process.* **Be sure to request accommodations well in advance of each semester.**
    □ *It is also the student's responsibility to meet with instructors and discuss accommodations approved by the school's DSO.* **Be sure to meet with instructors as soon as possible** (i.e., preferably within the first week of class) to discuss your accommodations.

  • **Be informed!** Meet with a representative from your school's DSO to discuss specifics of the process for securing and maintaining accommodations. Important things to know include:
    □ How often you must request accommodations (i.e., prior to the start of each semester?)
    □ How to pick up or access accommodation letters/documentation that can be distributed to your instructors

☐ Specific procedures for scheduling testing accommodations. Some instructors may be able to provide the needed testing accommodation (e.g., a testing environment free from distractions), but these accommodations may need to be provided through the school's DSO.

☐ Whom to contact if approved accommodations are not honored and provided

Reference: Americans with Disabilities Act of 1990. Public Law 101-336. 42 U.S.C. 12111, 12112 (1990). 2020

Appendix 2.6: Session 2 Handout

Emailing an Instructor

Emails between you and your instructors are professional communications. Use the steps below to make a good impression and portray yourself as a mature student.

- **Always use your university email address**
  - Your email address is the first thing your instructor will see and essentially makes the first impression.
  - Emails from personal email addresses may be ignored or directed to spam folders.
- **Subject lines should clearly and briefly state the purpose of your email.**
  - This is a good place to identify which of the instructor's classes you are in and the specific topic of the email. For example, "PSY 361 Midterm Paper" would be an appropriate subject line for an email containing questions about an upcoming assignment.
- **As always, address your instructor respectfully.**
  - When possible, you should locate your instructor's information on their faculty webpage. If your instructor has a Ph.D., Dr. "last name" is appropriate. If your instructor does not have a Ph.D., Ms. "last name" or Mr. "last name" is appropriate. When in doubt, overshoot! Address your instructor as Dr. "last name." If your instructor does not have a Ph.D., they may correct you but won't be offended.
- **Identify who you are and what class you are in.**
  - An opening statement such as, "My name is Jane Doe, and I am in your PSY 360 class," is one way to do this.
  - Alternatively, you can state what class you are emailing about in the body of your email and state your name in the closing.
- **Check your email for spelling and grammatical errors.**
  - This will convey to your instructor that you are an attentive and serious student.
- **DO NOT USE TXT-TALK!**
  - An email to your instructor is not a casual conversation with a friend. Text talk (i.e., "UR", "IDK", "btw," or "?4U") will be viewed as disrespectful and will portray you as a careless and ineffective communicator.
- **As with all communications between you and your instructor, you should ensure that you do not sound demanding.**
  - Be polite and respectful. Make requests, not demands.
  - Demands include statements like: "You need to meet with me tomorrow." A polite request would be similar to a statement such as: "I would like to schedule a meeting with you."

- **Use a formal closing when ending your emails.**
  - Formal closings include: "Sincerely," "Respectfully," "Best Wishes," and "Thank You." After the formal closing, type out your full name.

Reference: *Email Etiquette. (2020, July 1). The University of Southern Mississippi. Retrieved August 30, 2021, from click to see the linkclick to see the linkclick to see the linkclick to see the linkhttps://www.usm.edu/student-success/email-etiquette.php*

Appendix 2.7: Session 2 Homework

Effective Communication Worksheet

1) Set up a meeting with a faculty member to discuss strategies for success in their class or meet with a faculty member during their office hours.	
When was your meeting?	◆ Office Hours ◆ Scheduled time:
What specific concerns did you discuss with your instructor?	
2) Evaluate how the meeting went.	
What went well?	
What didn't go so well?	
List the instructor's suggestions or tips for success that you discussed during the meeting:	

Appendix 2.8: Session 2 Homework

Self-Rewards List

Table 2.2 Example Rewards List

Mini-Motivators (~10–15 minutes)	Small Rewards (~30–60 minutes)
Eat a piece of candy	Watch an episode of your favorite TV show
Read a short article in a magazine	Make an ice cream sundae
Play with your pet for a few minutes	Take a bubble bath
Listen to your favorite song	Take a walk around the neighborhood
Drink a cup of coffee	Call a friend
Medium rewards (~1–2 hours)	**Large rewards (Half or Full Day)**
Go to lunch with friends	Visit an out-of-town friend
Go to the movies	Plan a day trip to the beach
Play basketball with friends	Tailgate and attend a football game
Take a fun exercise class	Run in a 5K with a friend
Play videogames	
Give yourself a manicure	

Use Table 2.3 to create your own personalized rewards list. You can borrow rewards from the examples above and add your own. It is important that rewards be things you enjoy and will be motivated to work for. Try to identify more mini-motivators and small rewards than medium and large ones, as smaller rewards will be used more often.

Table 2.3 Personalized Rewards List

Mini-Motivators (~10–15 minutes)	Small Rewards (~30–60 minutes)

(Continued)

Table 2.3 (Continued)

Mini-Motivators (~10–15 minutes)	Small Rewards (~30–60 minutes)
Medium rewards (~1–2 hours)	Large rewards (Half or Full Day)

Appendix 2.9: Session 2 Homework

Self-Rewards Implementation Worksheet

Identify three to five tasks that you need to get done but tend to avoid. Assign rewards to these tasks and reward yourself when these tasks are completed (Table 2.4).

Table 2.4 Self-Rewards Worksheet

Task/Activity	Time Needed for Activity	Contingent Self-Reward
Example: Attending GOALS group	90 minutes	Watch a favorite TV show

What (if any) issues did you encounter when using self-rewards?

_____
_____
_____

Did you use any strategies to ensure that you followed through using self-rewards?

_____
_____

Chapter 3

Taking Notes From Lectures and Course Readings

Quick Look

Objective

Understand how to take thorough and helpful notes during class lectures, reading assignments, and other class-related activities.

Materials Needed

- ♦ Appendix 3.1: Session 3 Outline
- ♦ Appendix 3.2: Note-Taking Passage (Activity)
- ♦ Appendix 3.3: Blank Note Framework (Handout)
- ♦ Appendix 3.4: Note-Taking Example (Handout)
- ♦ *Optional:* Session 3 Fidelity Checklist (Table 3.1)

Session Highlights

- ♦ **Check-in**
  - • Discuss content covered in the previous session (i.e., self-advocacy, building motivation, and extracting information from a syllabus)
  - • Review previous session homework
- ♦ **Learn new skills**
  - • Actively listen and notice cues for important information during course lectures
  - • Take notes that thoroughly and efficiently capture class material (in both written and lecture format)
- ♦ **Wrap-up**
  - • Assign homework (complete notes using the strategies discussed during the session)
  - • Discuss content covered in the upcoming session

DOI: 10.4324/9781003199618-4

Detailed Session Content

Check-In

- ♦ Briefly review topics covered last week
  - Ask group members to summarize Session 2
  - Material covered during last session:
    - □ Effective communication with instructors (i.e., best practices for email communication, how to discuss tips for success, and classroom accommodations with instructors)
    - □ Contingent self-rewards (i.e., using rewards to motivate goal setting and attainment)
    - □ Extracting relevant information from a course syllabus
- ♦ Homework review
  - Appendix 2.7: Effective Communication Worksheet: group members contacted an instructor for a class in which they were having difficulties and documented how the meeting went.
  - Appendix 2.8: Self-reward list: group members were to add to their rewards list and categorize the newly added rewards according to size (i.e., small, medium, and large).
  - Appendix 2.9: Self-Rewards Worksheet: group members recorded tasks they needed to complete in the upcoming week and assigned a contingent reward for completing that task.
- ♦ Questions to facilitate group discussion:
  - Who was able to make an appointment and meet with their instructor?
  - What went well? What didn't go so well? What types of techniques did the instructor suggest?
  - What tasks/assignments were identified as targets for rewards? What rewards were assigned to these tasks?
  - Were there any barriers to using self-rewards? Any helpful strategies that you used to ensure that you would follow through with using self-rewards for these tasks?
  - Was everyone able to locate a course syllabus? Did you have trouble isolating the important information from the syllabus?

Skills Introduction: Taking Notes From Lectures and Course Readings

Describe

Learning how to take notes is a surprisingly complex process that involves several important steps. First, it is important to come to class prepared so that the material covered in class is not new, which makes following along and taking notes much easier. During class, the ability to listen and recognize when the instructor makes an important point is a skill that must be developed over time. It is also vital to learn how to take notes that capture all the necessary information from course lectures and readings. Finally, notes must be summarized and organized so that they can be used for test preparation.

Prepare

As discussed above, preparation outside of class is needed to facilitate thorough and efficient note-taking during class. This preparation should be inclusive of referring to the course syllabus to know what topics will be discussed in class, reading over course materials provided by the instructor (i.e., lecture outlines and learning objectives), and completing assigned readings. Oftentimes, there are review sections at the end of book chapters or on-line quizzes accessible via the textbook publisher, which are additional methods to become familiarized with the lecture material before each class.

Listen

There are two main types of listening: active and passive (Rogers & Farson, 1957). Passive listening involves listening without fully absorbing what the speaker is saying. For example, passive listening may occur when someone is working on another course assignment, scrolling through Instagram, or talking to a friend while the instructor is lecturing to the class. In contrast, active listening refers to thoughtfully listening to a speaker and hearing without judgment, as well as clarifying that information through restatements and questions (Topornycky & Golparian, 2016). In class, active listening occurs when a student focuses on the instructor, takes notes of important concepts, and asks questions when clarification is needed. It is also helpful to listen without judgment—if the content of what the instructor is saying is judged as uninteresting or boring, it may be easier to tune them out.

Tip for Group Leaders: Ask group members for examples of indications that an instructor is making an important point, writing the ones mentioned on the board. Then, provide the remaining examples to group members.

- Pausing
- Giving examples
- Making lists
- Repeating what has been said
- Quoting the textbook
- Changing volume or pitch of voice
- Spending considerable time on one concept
- Adding class activities or worksheets to reinforce or elaborate on a concept
- Using body language (e.g., facial expression, gestures, posture, and pace)
- Writing on the board
- Saying direct statements (e.g., "this is essential") or indicator words (e.g., significant, important, and most)

Take notes

There have been several strategies developed to help students capture information presented in lectures or course readings, so this material is ready for review when it is time to prepare for an upcoming exam or quiz. This section presents general strategies to keep in mind when taking notes, as well as a couple of methods of how to take notes in different formats.

General strategies

- Keep notes as short as possible—never use a sentence if you can use a phrase, and never use a phrase if you can use a word.
- Write notes in your own words, rather than trying to copy exactly what the instructor or book says.
- Use an outline form—indent subtopics, make lists, and use bullet points.
- If something is missed, write down key words and leave a blank space or circle it—this will serve as a reminder to get the information later from the instructor, another student, or the course textbook.
- Leave space in the margins in case there are concepts that are revisited in the lecture, a concept needs to be expanded upon, or an example is thought of that applies this concept to a real-life situation.
- Consider dating your notes and numbering the pages of these notes for organizational purposes.

Electronic note-taking strategy

Group members may choose to take notes electronically using applications such as Microsoft Word, Google Docs, Apple Notes, or OneNote. It is helpful to date your notes and give them a heading or title that matches the overarching topic discussed. The main notes section of the document should be used to paraphrase the details of what the instructor says in outline format. For example, it is important to write down not only the name of a term or concept, but also its definition and an example of how it may be applied. The comments section is used to pull out important concepts or key words, especially if the instructor makes note of its importance, so this information is easily found when preparing for tests. It may also be used to draft questions for the instructor or questions that can be answered by referring later to the course readings. A review section should come at the end of the main notes section that summarizes the lecture content in three to four sentences. It is recommended that the review section is completed shortly after class and after re-reading the lecture notes.

Handwritten note-taking strategy

A widely used method to take handwritten notes was developed by an education professor at Cornell University and subsequently has been termed the Cornell Note Taking System (The Learning Strategies Center, n.d.). According to this method, a single page is divided into three sections: a six-inch section on the right side of the page for in-class notes (e.g., important definitions of key terms or concepts and graphical representation of key terms or concepts). Then, a two-and-a-half-inch margin on the left side of the page is used for main ideas or prompts and may include topic headings, questions to be answered later, or reminders of key terms. A two-inch section on the bottom of the page is used to summarize the notes taken that day. For more information about the Cornell Note Taking System, navigate to the free online tutorial on their website.

Tip for Group Leaders: It may be helpful to print off some of the note-taking sheets provided by the Cornell Learning Strategies Center for group members who want to take paper notes.

Important tip: Instructors often provide their students with lecture outlines that are in PowerPoint or pdf format. These materials should be regarded as outlines and are not inclusive of all the information an instructor expects his/her students to know for an exam. It is vital that students make use of these outlines to follow along with the class lecture, but they must take their own notes to fill in the details (e.g., definitions or examples of terms). Additional information should be obtained from the course readings, and this information should also be extracted in note form by the student.

Demonstrate

Distribute copies of Appendix 3.2: Note-Taking Passage (Activity) to group members. Instruct group members to read the passage, underline the main concepts or ideas, and use Appendix 3.3: Blank Note Framework (Handout) to take notes. Group members may also take notes on their laptops, if applicable. After group members complete this exercise, have them share how they used this note-taking method to extract the important information from the passage, highlight the key concepts or terms, and summarize the overarching themes. Distribute a copy of Appendix 3.4: Note-Taking Example (Figure 3.1) to group members to provide a model of electronic notes for this passage may entail.

Discuss

Give group members the opportunity to ask questions about these note-taking strategies. Examples of questions to facilitate discussion include:

♦ What do you like about these note-taking methods?
♦ How do they compare to your current note-taking method?
♦ How might you implement one of these note-taking methods? Do you foresee any difficulties in implementing this plan?

Wrap-Up

♦ Give group members an opportunity to ask questions about the session's material.
♦ Session review: Topics covered during this session included:

- • Actively listening during lectures
- • Taking notes effectively from lectures and reading assignments
- ♦ Homework: Group members are asked to take notes for one class using the methods discussed during this session. This can be lecture notes or notes on a reading assignment. These will be reviewed next week, and the group members given feedback.
- ♦ Remind group members of the next session time, place, and topics to be covered.
  - • Group members will learn about time awareness and mindfulness in the next session.

Table 3.1 Session 3 Fidelity Checklist

Task	Rating		
	0	1	2
Prepared materials for the session (i.e., printed handouts for all group members)			
Reviewed topics covered at the previous session			
Discussed homework assignment from the previous session			
Offered opportunity for group members to ask questions about the previous session			
Asked group members for examples of indicators an instructor is making an important point			
Provided information about different types of note-taking, including paper notes, electronic notes, and PowerPoint notes			
Asked questions to assess group members understanding of this skill and to promote engagement			
Offered opportunity for group members to ask questions about the current session			
Assigned homework based on the topic covered during this session			
Mentioned date and topic of the next session			

0—Group Leader did not execute task.
1—Group Leader partially executed task.
2—Group Leader fully executed task.

References

The Learning Strategies Center. (n.d.). https://lsc.cornell.edu/how-to-study/taking-notes/cornell-note-taking-system/

Rogers, C.R., & Farson, R.E. (1957). Active listening.

Topornycky, J., & Golparian, S. (2016). Balancing openness and interpretation in active listening. *Collected Essays on Learning and Teaching*, 9, 175–184.

Appendix 3.1: Session 3 Outline

Taking Notes From Lectures and Course Readings

Prepare

♦ Preparation outside of class is needed to facilitate thorough and efficient note-taking during class. This preparation should be inclusive of referring to the course syllabus to know what topics will be discussed in class, reading over course materials provided by the instructor (i.e., lecture outlines and learning objectives), and completing assigned readings.

♦ Oftentimes, there are review sections at the end of book chapters or on-line quizzes accessible via the textbook publisher, which are additional methods to become familiarized with the lecture material before each class.

Listen

♦ Active listening involves listening to a speaker and hearing without judgment, as well as clarifying that information through restatements and questions. In class, active listening occurs when a student focuses on the instructor, takes notes of important concepts, and ask questions when clarification is needed. Here are some examples of ways to know that an instructor is making an important point:
  - Pausing
  - Giving examples
  - Making lists
  - Repeating what has been said
  - Quoting the textbook
  - Changing volume or pitch of voice
  - Spending considerable time on one concept
  - Adding class activities or worksheets to reinforce or elaborate on a concept
  - Using body language (e.g., facial expression, gestures, posture, and pace)
  - Writing on the board
  - Saying direct statements (e.g., "this is essential") or indicator words (e.g., significant and important, most)

Take Notes

♦ Keep notes as short as possible—never use a sentence if you can use a phrase, and never use a phrase if you can use a word.

- Write notes in your own words, rather than trying to copy exactly what the instructor or book says.
- Use an outline form—indent subtopics, make lists, and use bullet points.
- If something is missed, write down key words and leave a blank space or circle it—this will serve as a reminder to get the information later from the instructor, another student, or the course textbook.
- Leave space in the margins in case there are concepts that are revisited in the lecture, a concept needs to be expanded upon, or an example is thought of that applies this concept to a real-life situation.
- Consider dating your notes and number the pages of these notes for organizational purposes.

Appendix 3.2: Session 3 Activity

Note-Taking Passage

Mitosis is a vital process for growth and cell replacement in multicelled organisms. Additionally, in certain organisms (e.g., protists, fungi, and some animals and plants), mitosis is a form of asexual reproduction. Mitosis involves four primary phases: prophase, metaphase, anaphase, and telophase.

Prophase includes early prophase and late prophase. In early prophase, the cell begins going through mitosis. In late prophase, the centrioles in the cell begin separating and the nuclear envelope starts to break up and dissipate. Next, the cell goes through metaphase. The nuclear envelope is completely eliminated during the transition into metaphase. Additionally, the centrioles move to opposite poles of the cell and spindle fibers attach to chromosomes via the kinetochore. Anaphase comes next. During this phase of mitosis, the spindle fibers are shortened, chromosomes separate, and non-kinetochore fibers length, pushing poles away from one another. Finally, telophase occurs. This is when the cells fully separate and the chromosomes within each of the cells de-condense.

Simultaneously, during late anaphase, the process of cytokinesis begins and continues until after telophase. There are two mechanisms involved in cytokinesis: cell plate formation (in plants) and cleavage (in animals). Cell plate formation occurs when the Golgi bodies send vesicles to the midpoint of the cell, which forms the cell membrane. These vesicles are full of enzymes, which deposit the cellulose needed to create the cell wall. In animal cells, cleavage involves a ring of actin and myosin, which forms a "belt" on the inside of the cell. As this "belt" contacts, it pulls the plasma membrane along with it, allowing cytokinesis to occur.

This cycle is controlled by the G1 checkpoint and the G2 checkpoint. Notably, the G1 checkpoint is implicated in the development of some cancers. This is because suppressor proteins (which stop the process through the cell cycle) are mutated in cancer, causing cells to grow and divide uncontrollably. Proto-oncogenes are normal genes that mutate into oncogenes, or cancer-causing genes.

Appendix 3.3: Session 3 Handout

Blank Note Framework

Date: _____

Title: _____

    I. Major Topic:
       A. Sub-topic:
       B. Sub-topic
   II. Major Topic:
       A. Sub-topic:
       B. Sub-topic
  III. Major Topic:
       A. Sub-topic:
       B. Sub-topic
  IV. Summary of Session

Appendix 3.4: Session 3 Handout

Note-Taking Example

Figure 3.1 Note-Taking Example Handout

> Add date and title to the top of your notes

Notes from February 2
A Closer Look at Mitosis
- Multi-celled organisms:
  - Growth
  - Cell replacement
- Protists, fungi, some animals and plants
  - Asexual reproduction

Laura Hansen
Phases of Mitosis—will be on the test, per instructor!

Prophase
Early Prophase: cell begins mitosis
Late prophase: chromosomes become more compact
- Beginning of the break-up of the nuclear envelope
- Centrioles start to separate

Metaphase
Transition to metaphase: nuclear envelope is gone
- Centrioles move to opposite poles
- Spindle fibers attach to chromosomes via the kinetochore

> Use comments for key words and phrases, or concepts for follow-up

Anaphase
- Spindle fibers are shortened
- Chromosomes separate
- Non-kinetochore fibers-lengthen, pushing poles away from one another

Laura Hansen
Ask instructor: what's the difference between Kinetochore & Nonkinetochore?

Telophase
- Cells separate
- Chromosomes de-condense

Cytokinesis
- Starts during late anaphase→continues until after telophase
- 2 mechanisms:
  - Cell plate formation in plants
  - Cleavage in animals
- Cell plate formation – Golgi sends vesicles to midpoint of cell→form a cell membrane
  - Vesicles are full of enzymes: deposit cellulose to create a cell wall
- Cleavage – the ring of actin and myosin forms a "belt" on the inside of the cell
  - Begins to contract→pulls the plasma membrane with it

Laura Hansen
Golgi bodies—add more information from the textbook

What controls the cycle
- G1 checkpoint and G2 checkpoint
- G1 checkpoint – involved in cancer
  - Suppressor proteins stop procession through the cell cycle
  - In cancer, suppressors are mutated→cells grow and divide uncontrollably
- Proto-oncogenes: normal genes that mutate into oncogenes (cancer-causing genes)

> After each class, briefly summarize the information at the end of your notes

SUMMARY
- Mitosis includes prophase, metaphase, anaphase, and telophase. It is controlled by G1 and G2 checkpoints.
- Proto-oncogenes are when normal cells become cancers cells

Chapter 4

Time Awareness and Tuning Out Distractions

Quick Look

Objectives

- ◆ Learn how to estimate how long daily tasks take to develop efficient schedules.
- ◆ Define the concept of mindfulness and learn targeted mindfulness techniques to improve focus and tune out distractions.

Materials Needed

- ◆ Appendix 4.1: Session 4 Outline
- ◆ Appendix 4.2: Time Awareness Word Search (Activity)
- ◆ Appendix 4.3: Mindfulness Exercises (Handout)
- ◆ Appendix 4.4: Time Awareness Worksheet (Homework)
- ◆ Appendix 4.5: Mindfulness Practice (Homework)
- ◆ *Optional:* Session 4 Fidelity Checklist (Table 4.1)

Session Highlights

- ◆ Check-in
  - • Discuss content covered in the previous session (taking notes from lectures and reading assignments)
  - • Review previous session homework (note-taking practice)
- ◆ Learn new skills
  - • Improving time awareness
  - • Managing distractions
- ◆ Wrap-up
  - • Assign homework (time awareness practice and mindfulness rehearsal)
  - • Discuss content covered in the upcoming session

DOI: 10.4324/9781003199618-5

Detailed Session Content
Check-In

♦ Briefly review topics covered during the last session
  • Ask group members to summarize Session 3
  • Material covered during the last session:
    □ Actively listening during course lectures
    □ Strategies for taking notes during lectures and from readings
♦ Homework review
  • Group members were asked to take notes during a class lecture or on a reading homework assignment
♦ Questions to facilitate group discussion:
  • Which note-taking strategy did you choose? Why?
  • What went well as you implemented your strategy? What barriers did you encounter?

Tip for Group Leaders: Ask group members if they are willing to show and share their notes with one another. It can be helpful for group members to visualize the different ways that the note-taking strategies discussed during this previous session can be put into practice!

Skills Introduction: Time Awareness
Describe

The perception that time is passing too quickly is often a great source of stress and is most likely a source of difficulty for members in this group. With practice, time may become a more manageable part of life instead of a perplexing force that seems beyond our control.

Time awareness is a fundamental skill that allows for the planning, organization, and prioritization of academic and personal responsibilities. Paying close attention to how much time has passed as daily tasks are completed improves the ability to accurately estimate how much time is needed to complete tasks. It also facilitates the creation of daily schedules. Importantly, once the time needed to complete obligations is known, there will be more time to spend with family, friends, and doing things that are enjoyable. To master time awareness, it is crucial to have constant access to a time tracking device.

Demonstrate

Distribute Appendix 4.2 Time Awareness Word Search (Figure 4.1). Ask group members to estimate how long it will take them to complete the task. Record these time estimates and ask group members to write them down at the top of the handout. Start the task and begin timing. Ask group members to write down the time it took for them to actually complete the task.

Discuss

Questions to encourage group discussion:

♦ Was there a difference between the estimated time and the actual time it took to complete the task?
♦ Did you find that you overestimated or underestimated the time it would take?
♦ Do you tend to run into the same kinds of problems when scheduling your study time and completing course assignments?

Skills Introduction: Mindfulness
Describe

Mindfulness is a "state of consciousness" that involves focusing on moment-to-moment experiences (Shapiro et al., 2006). Mindful practice originated with Eastern religious traditions, particularly Buddhism, whose practitioners often seek to achieve mindfulness through intensive meditation. Several activities and techniques promote mindfulness, including yoga, tai chi, and meditation. Mindfulness has been shown to boost working memory, reduce stress, and improve focus, among other things, and has been used by sports teams and the military to enhance performance. Additionally, techniques such as Mindfulness-Based Stress Reduction and Mindful Studying have recently gained popularity as strategies for improving academic performance. The integration of mindfulness into the Group for Organization and Learning Skills (GOALS) is designed to help group members learn how to focus on the task-at-hand and tune out distractions.

Explain to group members that they will know when they mastered a mindfulness activity if they infrequently or no longer need to redirect their mind during the activity. At this point, they should move on to a new, more challenging mindfulness activity.

Demonstrate

Focus on a single minute is an activity meant to help group members become aware of their internal sense of time by allowing them to see if they are estimating time the way they think they are. This activity is also an opportunity to introduce group members to one way of practicing mindfulness. Group members should be encouraged to notice and accept their thoughts and then gently guide their attention back to the present moment when completing this activity.

Focus on a single minute:

Close your eyes, sit up straight in your chair with your feet on the floor.
Focus on breathing in and out slowly and deliberately.
Raise your hand when you think a minute has passed but keep your eyes closed.
Keep it up for a few seconds and then you can put it back down.
[After all group members have raised their hands.]
You may slowly open your eyes and return your focus to the group.

Group leaders should mark down the time each group member raises their hand.

Discuss

Ask each group member to estimate how much time had passed when they raised their hand, then tell them how much time had actually passed. Discuss if they overestimated or under-estimated the passage of one minute, or if they were close to their estimates.

Suggestions for group discussion:

♦ Were you surprised by the accuracy/inaccuracy with which you estimated a single minute?
♦ What implications does this activity have for your time awareness?
♦ Did you find this easier or harder than the previous time estimation activity (i.e., word search or maze)? Why?
♦ Some people think time passes quickly, so they rush to do things and then immediately start thinking of the next task. Other people feel time passes very slowly, so they often believe that they have more time to complete a task than they actually do. Based on this activity, which type of person are you and how does it impact your level of stress?

During this discussion, highlight the importance of daily mindfulness practice, as this will be vital to building this skill. Solicit examples of activities during which group members can practice mindfulness in their daily lives. Group leaders may suggest beginning with an easier mindfulness activity such as breathing mindfully, eating mindfully, or mindfully engaging in a mundane task (e.g., washing the dishes, sweeping the floor, brushing teeth, and walking to class). It is also recommended that group members keep their mindfulness exercises short (five to ten minutes). Mindfulness is akin to a muscle and stamina must be built over time.

Distribute Appendix 4.3: Mindfulness Exercises (Handout). Ask group members which mindfulness activities they plan to use, when they plan to use them, and why they plan to use them.

Wrap-Up

♦ Briefly review topics discussed during this session and ask group members if they have any questions about the session content

- ◆ Distribute session outline (Appendix 4.1)
- ◆ Assign homework
  - • Appendix 4.4: Time Awareness Worksheet: write down a list of assignments and how much time is needed to complete each assignment.
  - • Appendix 4.5: Mindfulness Practice: complete one or two mindfulness activities and write a short paragraph (three to five sentences) about this experience.
- ◆ Remind group members of the next session time, place, and topics to be covered:
  - • Session 5: Prioritizing and Scheduling Tasks

Table 4.1 Session 4 Fidelity Checklist

Task	Rating		
	0	1	2
Prepared materials for the session (i.e., printed handouts for all group members)			
Reviewed topics covered at the previous session			
Discussed homework assignment from the previous session			
Offered opportunity for group members to ask questions about the previous session			
Instructed group members to write down time estimated for word search or maze			
Identified group members as "Underestimators" or "Overestimators"			
Completed mindfulness activity			
Asked questions to assess group members understanding of skills and to promote engagement			
Offered opportunity for group members to ask questions about the current session			
Assigned homework based on the topic covered during this session			
Mentioned date and topic of the next session			
Reviewed topics covered at the previous session			

0—Group Leader did not execute task.
1—Group Leader partially executed task.
2—Group Leader fully executed task.

References

Author Unknown. Free mindfulness. http://www.freemindfulness.org/
Author Unknown. Greater Good in Action: Science-Based Practices for a Meaningful Life. https://ggia.berkeley.edu/practice/raisin_meditation
Shapiro, S.L., Carlson, L.E., Astin, J.A., & Freedman, B. (2006). Mechanisms of mindfulness. *Journal of Clinical Psychology, 62*, 373–386.

Appendix 4.1: Session 4 Outline

Time Awareness and Tuning Out Distractions

Time Awareness

♦ The passage of time may be a source of great stress for you (e.g., not having enough time in the day to get everything done), but—with practice—time can become a more manageable part of your life.

♦ Why is time awareness such an important skill?
  • It allows you to plan, organize, and prioritize your responsibilities.
  • It is the first step in effectively managing your time.

♦ Practicing is essential to fully develop this skill!

What are some effective ways to practice and improve time awareness?

♦ Estimate how much time you anticipate needing to complete various activities (e.g., washing the dishes, getting dressed, writing a paper, and studying for a test) and write your time estimation down. After completing each activity, compare the actual time it took you to complete the task to the estimated time. With continued use, this exercise will help you become more accurate in estimating the completion of other tasks.

♦ Remember, constant access to a time tracking device is crucial to developing good time awareness.
  • While cell phones have a clock and are usually with us, they can be very distracting and can easily turn into a method of procrastination.
  • Try using a watch instead. A watch is always handy and is much less distracting than cell phones. You can also turn off notifications on your phone temporarily by putting it in "Do Not Disturb" mode.

Mindfulness

♦ Mindfulness is a moment-to-moment awareness of our lived experience without judgment.

♦ It has been shown to boost working memory, reduce stress, and improve focus, among other things.

♦ As you begin practicing mindfulness exercises, keep in mind the following:
  • Begin with easier activities such as breathing mindfully or mindfully engaging in a mundane, everyday task.
  • Keep your mindfulness exercises short (i.e., five to ten minutes) and if your mind wanders, simply notice and accept your thoughts and then gently guide your attention back to the present moment.

- Mastery of a mindfulness activity usually occurs when you notice a dramatic decrease in how often you need to re-direct your attention to the task-at-hand. When you reach this level of skill, move on to a new, more challenging mindfulness activity (e.g., alternating between focusing on your internal feelings/thoughts to what you see, hear, or feel in the outside world).

Appendix 4.2: Session 4 Handout

Time Awareness Word Search

Figure 4.1 Time Awareness Word Search

```
A  B  G  P  D  L  C  O  M  M  U  N  I  C  A  T  I  O  N  Q
C  D  H  R  E  M  J  H  P  O  E  M  N  U  H  S  Q  P  L  W
C  E  R  T  F  Q  K  J  X  Y  S  T  R  A  T  E  G  Y  P  E
O  K  F  E  S  T  I  M  A  T  E  P  E  K  E  R  H  M  W  R
M  G  T  U  T  K  E  K  C  U  A  R  T  M  R  T  J  N  E  T
P  H  T  V  Y  W  I  L  V  I  S  T  Y  L  T  Y  K  O  T  Y
L  F  V  B  Z  E  G  L  B  O  D  E  U  Z  Y  U  L  X  R  U
I  K  U  N  X  R  H  W  L  R  E  S  P  O  N  S  I  B  L  E
S  M  I  Y  C  T  P  E  N  O  F  X  I  X  U  I  Z  D  R  I
H  E  V  M  V  Y  R  R  M  U  G  C  O  C  I  O  X  A  P  O
M  O  W  O  P  U  T  A  T  T  E  N  D  A  N  C  W  J  U  E
E  P  Q  T  B  R  E  J  Q  I  I  V  O  V  O  A  C  E  N  F
N  O  R  I  N  I  S  K  W  M  J  M  A  T  R  P  V  R  C  F
T  S  X  V  M  O  S  V  R  E  W  A  R  D  E  A  B  T  T  O
C  T  P  A  L  P  E  L  E  P  L  Q  S  N  A  S  N  S  U  R
X  U  L  T  K  A  C  G  F  H  J  M  D  M  S  D  S  P  A  T
W  F  V  E  J  S  C  E  T  Q  P  K  F  Q  E  L  M  R  L  P
V  Q  M  Q  H  D  U  R  R  F  Z  W  G  W  A  F  Q  T  U  L
P  R  O  F  E  S  S  I  O  N  A  L  H  O  M  G  W  E  Q  M
B  Y  P  R  F  C  V  W  S  H  O  R  G  A  N  I  Z  E  X  N
```

1. ACCOMPLISHMENT
2. ATTEND
3. AWARE
4. COMMUNICATION
5. EFFORT
6. ESTIMATE
7. GOALS
8. MOTIVATE
9. ORGANIZE
10. PROFESSIONAL
11. PUNCTUAL
12. RESPONSIBLE
13. REWARD
14. SKILL
15. SUCCESS
16. TIME

Appendix 4.3: Session 4 Handout

Mindfulness Exercises

Note: Each mindfulness exercise should take approximately five to ten minutes. You may wish to digitally record these instructions and play them as you complete each exercise.

Recognizing Your Body and Surroundings

(credit: https://www.padraigomorain.com**, as posted on freemindfulness.org/download). An audio version of this exercise is also available on the website.**

1. Notice your breathing. No need to breathe in a particular way, just notice the fact that you are breathing.
2. Notice your posture—whether you are sitting down, lying down, standing, or walking.
3. Notice points of contact between your body and the chair, or perhaps your body and the bed.
4. Notice the feeling of your clothes against your skin, perhaps the feeling of your feet against the soles of your shoes.
5. Now, notice the sounds around you. First, notice sounds from within the space that you are in. Now, notice sounds from outside the space that you are in. Now, notice the sound furthest away from you that you can hear.
6. Now, return to noticing your breathing for a time, but whenever thoughts cross your mind, return gently to your breathing.
7. Refocus on your surroundings and return your attention to whatever you were doing prior to this exercise.

Mindfully Eating a Piece of Fruit

Modified from https://ggia.berkeley.edu/practice/raisin_meditation

Examples of Fruit to Use:

- ♦ Apple slice
- ♦ Orange slice
- ♦ Banana slice
- ♦ Grape or raisin

Holding/Seeing

First, pick up the piece of food and hold it between your finger and thumb or in your palm. Fully direct your focus onto the piece of food. Allow your eyes to explore every aspect of the food, examining where the light hits the item, where there are shadows, and any imperfections in the item (e.g., dents, ridges, and bumps).

Touching

Investigate the texture of the food with your fingers. Notice the moisture, dryness, grit, etc. It may be helpful to close your eyes for this step to hone your focus.

Smelling

Hold the food beneath your nose and inhale slowly. As you inhale, focus solely on the aroma as it enters your nostrils. Notice any changes to your body as this happens (e.g., stomach rumbling, mouth watering).

Engaging

Now, slowly bring the food up to your lips and gently place the food on your tongue. Notice how the texture changes in your mouth and explore the food with your tongue, taking your time before chewing.

Tasting

Notice your body's impulse to start chewing, and when you are ready, take one or two purposeful bites. Note what happens after you chew, perceiving changes in the taste, texture, and reaction in your mouth as you continue to chew. Before swallowing, consider the sensation in your mouth as the food continues to change over time, as well as how your mouth and body are responding to the presence of the foods.

Swallowing

Next, when you feel ready, swallow the food. Notice the urge to swallow and then carry it out with intention, so that you are aware of every step of this process.

Concluding

Lastly, follow the food as it courses through your body. Notice how your body feels after completing this exercise. Observe the urges and impulses your body has as you slowly come back to consciousness of your environment.

Appendix 4.4: Session 4 Homework

Time Awareness Worksheet

In Table 4.2, make a list of class assignments due in the next few weeks. If necessary, break down larger assignments into smaller tasks, which may each occupy their own line in the table. Next, estimate how long each task or assignment will take (rounded to the nearest half-hour). Finally, record how long it actually took to complete the assignment.

Table 4.2 Time Awareness Worksheet

Assignment	Due Date	Estimated Time	Actual Time
Read two chapters for intro to psych	April 2	30 minutes	75 minutes
Assignment	**Due Date**	**Estimated Time**	**Actual Time**

Appendix 4.5: Session 4 Homework

Mindfulness Practice

Activity 1

Which mindfulness activity did you practice?

_____

How long were you engaged in this activity?

_____

Write a paragraph summarizing your experience practicing this mindfulness activity (e.g., What did you learn? How was this mindfulness exercise helpful? What aspect of this exercise was difficult? What strategies did you use to make the mindfulness activity easier?).

_____
_____
_____
_____
_____

Activity 2

Which mindfulness activity did you practice?

_____

How long were you engaged in this activity?

_____

Write a paragraph summarizing your experience practicing this mindfulness activity (e.g., What did you learn? How was this mindfulness exercise helpful? What aspect of this exercise was difficult? What strategies did you use to make the mindfulness activity easier?).

_____
_____
_____
_____
_____

Chapter 5

Prioritizing and Scheduling Tasks

Quick Look

Objectives

♦ Group members will learn how to develop to-do lists and prioritize tasks.
♦ Group members will learn how to schedule course-related tasks and other important events using a planner or calendar.

Materials Needed

♦ Appendix 5.1: Session 5 Outline
♦ Appendix 5.2: Printable Calendar Page (Handout)
♦ Appendix 5.3: Listing and Prioritizing Tasks (Homework)
♦ *Optional:* Session 5 Fidelity Checklist (Table 5.1)

Session Highlights

♦ Check-in
  • Discuss content covered in the previous session (Time Awareness and Tuning Out Distractions)
  • Review Session 4 homework (Time Awareness Worksheet and Mindfulness Practice)
♦ Learn new skills
  • List and prioritize tasks
  • Schedule tasks using a planner
♦ Wrap-up
  • Assign homework (listing and prioritizing tasks)
  • Discuss content covered in the upcoming session

DOI: 10.4324/9781003199618-6

Detailed Session Content

Check-In

- ♦ Briefly review topics covered last week.
  - Ask group members to summarize Session 4
  - Material covered during the last session:
    - □ Group members learned whether they tend to overestimate or underestimate the amount of time needed to complete assignments, as well as how to use that awareness to plan for upcoming assignments.
    - □ Group members learned mindfulness-based strategies to promote focus and situational awareness.
  - Answer questions concerning the material presented in the previous session
- ♦ Homework review
  - Review Time Awareness Worksheet:
    - □ Comment on any trends that are seen for each group member with respect to the accuracy of their time estimations. Remember to differentiate between under-estimators and overestimators and how that might impact the completion of tasks:
      - Underestimators: Group members who do not give themselves enough time to complete a given task.
      - Overestimators: Group members who give themselves too much time to complete a given task.
  - Ask group members to volunteer reading their paragraph that summarizes their experience practicing a mindfulness activity.

Skills Introduction: Listing and Prioritizing Tasks

Ask group members how they keep track of tasks they need to complete each day. Do they use to-do lists, follow the class syllabus schedule, or use a planner? Are there different strategies they use for short- vs. long-term tasks or assignments?

To-Do Lists

Developing daily to-do lists is an important aspect of time management and planning. To-do lists provide structure, especially to long, uninterrupted periods of time, and promote a sense of accomplishment. In addition, it is useful to have to-do lists so that contingent self-rewards (discussed in Session 2) may be assigned to tasks. It is important to update to-do lists as tasks are completed as well as retain tasks that are not yet completed and add new tasks on the next day's to-do list. To-do lists should be completed each night for the following day or first thing in the morning, increasing the likelihood that to-do lists will be used.

Prioritizing Tasks

An important aspect of using to-do lists is prioritizing tasks to be completed. While there may be several things to accomplish on a to-do list, some tasks might need to be completed quickly while others could be delayed. Further, some tasks may take precedence over others because of their level of importance. It may be a good idea to consider long- and short-term goals when prioritizing tasks, considering such an approach will promote the achievement of these goals. As mentioned previously, priorities may change from moment-to-moment or day-to-day so the updating of to-do lists and the prioritization of tasks should be done continuously.

The **Important/Urgent diagram** (also known as the Eisenhower Matrix) is one method for prioritizing tasks. It is presented graphically as a diagram subdivided into four quadrants: important and urgent, important and not urgent, not important and urgent, and not important and not urgent. All tasks from a to-do list fall into one of these four quadrants and the highest priority should be given to the important and not urgent quadrant, as this facilitates long-term planning and goal-setting. The goal of this system is to help guide the sequence of tasks and to ensure that not too much time is given to tasks that are not vital to long-term goals or are considered distractions (i.e., not important and not urgent).

Group leaders should reproduce the Important/Urgent diagram (e.g., on a whiteboard or projector) so that it is viewable to all group members as this concept is explained (Figure 5.1).

Important/Urgent Diagram

Figure 5.1 Important/Urgent Diagram (adapted from Stephen Covey's *The Seven Habits of Highly Effective People*, 1989).

Important AND Urgent Example: studying for an exam that will be taken tomorrow	**Not Important AND Urgent** Example: responding to text messages from friends
Important AND Not Urgent Example: completing a term paper due the last week of the semester	**Not Important AND Not Urgent** Example: cleaning out the sock drawer

♦ **Important and urgent**—tasks such as tests or assignments that are due within the next few days

♦ **Important but not urgent**—tasks with the highest priority level, such as long-term projects or papers that contribute a great deal to the overall course grade

♦ **Not important but urgent**—demands that come up frequently throughout the day and tend to interrupt the completion of other tasks or obligations, such as emails or text messages

♦ **Not important and not urgent**—tasks with the lowest priority level and may involve "someday" or avoidance activities, such as reorganizing your closet or shopping online for unessential items

Demonstrate

Instruct group members to make a to-do list of five to ten things they need to accomplish in the next few days. These should be tasks from various aspects of their lives, not just limited to course-related work. For example, encourage group members to include job responsibilities and social activities, as well as general daily living tasks (e.g., doing laundry and cleaning room). Solicit examples from group members of tasks they have written down and list them so they are visible to everyone. Ask group members to prioritize these tasks using the Important/Urgent diagram.

Discuss

♦ Solicit from group members examples of how they might apply this skill in their daily lives.

♦ Ask group members to evaluate this strategy. The following questions may be used to prompt discussion:

• What might facilitate their use of this skill?

• What challenges might arise when implementing this strategy? How could they overcome these challenges?

Skills Introduction: Scheduling Tasks Using a Planner

Following the prioritization of tasks on to-do lists, another important step is adding these tasks to a planner. Using a planner provides structure to each day by helping establish a schedule and decreases the likelihood of forgetting to complete required tasks. While this practice may feel like an unnecessary extra step, it serves as another reminder to get important and urgent tasks done and gives guidance on how to be successful across every aspect of life (e.g., school, work, and social obligations).

Here are some general strategies of how and when to use planners or calendars for scheduling:

1. Choose either a paper or electronic planner or calendar. Oftentimes, colleges and universities have free or low-cost planners or calendars available at the beginning of

each semester that already include notable dates (e.g., finals week and last day to add/drop classes). Every smartphone and most email platforms have a calendar where recurring events can be added.

2. Write down or program recurring tasks in a planner or calendar at the beginning of each semester (e.g., schedule electricity bill payments at the same time each month, recurring class times, and work schedules).

3. Record due dates for tests and assignments once a course syllabus becomes available.

4. Plan portions of time to do difficult or challenging activities (e.g., writing a paper and completing a large amount of reading) when motivation is the highest. Make sure to also schedule time for contingent self-rewards as applicable.

5. Make use of breaks in a schedule or brief instances of downtime (e.g., commute to class and time waiting for a coffee order) to accomplish small tasks such as making a to-do list, planning out when to complete these tasks, or brainstorming a topic for a paper.

6. Be sure to schedule time for relaxation throughout the week and on weekends as a reward for all the hard work!

Demonstrate

Distribute Appendix 5.2: Printable Calendar Page (Table 5.2) to group members. This handout, an electronic calendar on their phones, or an already owned and available paper planner may be used for this activity. Instruct group members to add important dates to their calendars or planners for the upcoming week. If they are unsure of what to add, group members may refer to the to-do list they developed earlier in the session and then add these items to their planners or calendar. They can also use their homework sheet from the previous session.

Tip for Group Leaders: There is a wide variety of what types of planners group members may choose to use. It is recommended that you encourage group members to decide which type of planner they are going to use so that they can use it for the remainder of the program. Additionally, if they choose to use printable calendar pages, we recommend encouraging them to use a folder or binder to keep track of them.

Discuss

Use the following questions to encourage discussion about how group members intend to use this skill:

♦ Which type of calendar or planner do group members plan to use?

♦ How will group members make use of their planners? For schoolwork, jobs, and/or social activities?

♦ How might this strategy help overcome some of the challenges group members face when determining work schedules or when trying to get their coursework done on time?

♦ What other options might be used to schedule daily tasks and activities besides paper and electronic planners?

Wrap-Up

♦ Allow group members to ask questions about this session's content
♦ Distribute Appendix 5.1: Session 5 Outline to group members
♦ Assign homework
   • Appendix 5.3: Listing and Prioritizing Tasks (Table 5.3)
      □ Make a to-do list for the upcoming week, assign priority levels to each task, and then record whether or not it was added to a calendar or planner
♦ Remind group members of the next session time, place, and topics to be covered:
   • Session 6: Program Review and Organizing Your Workspace
      □ Group leaders will review the strategies covered so far during the GOALS program and reinforce the skills taught in Sessions 1 through 5. They will have the chance to discuss the successes and challenges they faced while implementing these skills. Group members will also learn how to organize their workspace and course materials to enhance their productivity and focus.

Table 5.1 Session 5 Fidelity Checklist

Task	Rating		
	0	1	2
Prepared materials for the session (i.e., printed handouts for all group members)			
Reviewed topics covered at the previous session			
Discussed homework assignment from the previous session			
Offered opportunity for group members to ask questions about the previous session			
Wrote the Important/Urgent diagram on the board and solicited examples for each category			
Asked each group member what type of planner they are going to use			
Asked questions to assess group members understanding of this skill and to promote engagement			
Offered opportunity for group members to ask questions about the current session			
Assigned homework based on the topic covered during this session			
Mentioned date and topic of the next session			

0—Group Leader did not execute task.
1—Group Leader partially executed task.
2—Group Leader fully executed task.

Reference

Covey, S.R. (1989). *The seven habits of highly effective people: Restoring the character Ethic: 7 habits of highly effective people.* Simon & Schuster.

Appendix 5.1: Session 5 Outline

Prioritizing and Scheduling Tasks

Listing and Prioritizing Tasks

- Use a daily to-do list to determine what tasks need to be accomplished.
- Update this list each day, noting what you accomplished and what still needs to be done.
- Assign a level of importance and a level of urgency to different tasks on your to-do list so you know what to prioritize and what to get done.
  - **Important and urgent**—tasks such as tests or assignments that are due within the next few days
  - **Important but not urgent**—tasks with the highest priority level, such as long-term projects or papers that contribute a great deal to the overall course grade
  - **Not important but urgent**—demands that come up frequently throughout the day and tend to interrupt the completion of other tasks or obligations (e.g., emails and text messages)
  - **Not important and not urgent**—tasks with the lowest priority level and may involve "someday" or avoidance activities (e.g., reorganizing the closet)

Strategies for Prioritizing Tasks

- Before beginning a block of work, prioritize the tasks you need to complete.
  - Use the Important/Urgent diagram to help guide your priorities.
- Attempt to use large, uninterrupted periods of time for activities that require a high level of concentration and focus.
- It may be helpful to categorize tasks according to similar characteristics (e.g., length of time needed for completion, level of effort, and subject area).
- Priorities may change from moment-to-moment or day-to-day—consider your short and long-term goals when determining what to focus on.
- Mini-motivators (i.e., small and time-limited rewards) will help you work consistently but remain motivated.
- If necessary, schedule simpler, more enjoyable tasks as rewards for completing more demanding or difficult tasks.
- Start with something that requires less concentration or a task you find easier or more doable.

Using a Planner to Schedule Tasks

- Write down or program recurring tasks in your planner at the beginning of each semester (e.g., schedule your electricity bill payment at the same time each month).

- Record due dates for tests and assignments once you receive a class syllabus.
- Plan times to do difficult or challenging activities when you know your motivation will be the highest.
- Schedule larger blocks of time for tasks that require a great deal of mental effort (e.g., writing a paper and completing a large amount of reading).
- Make use of breaks in your day (e.g., waiting for your next class and commuting to campus) to accomplish small tasks (i.e., make a to-do list, brainstorm a topic for a paper, and make an appointment).
- Be sure to schedule time for relaxation throughout the week and on weekends as a reward for your hard work.

Appendix 5.2: Session 5 Handout

Table 5.2 Printable Calendar Page

Time	Monday	Tuesday	Wednesday	Thursday	Friday	Saturday/Sunday
8:00 AM						
9:00 AM						
10:00 AM						
11:00 AM						
12:00 PM						
1:00 PM						
2:00 PM						
3:00 PM						
4:00 PM						
5:00 PM						

TASKS FOR THIS WEEK

_____   _____

_____   _____

_____   _____

_____   _____

_____

Appendix 5.3: Session 5 Homework

Listing and Prioritizing Tasks

Table 5.3 Session 5 Homework

Task	Priority Level	Put in Planner? Y/N
Example: read chapter one of math textbook by Wednesday	Important and Urgent	Y

Chapter 6

Program Review and Getting Organized

Quick Look

Objectives

♦ Group members will review skills they have learned so far in the Group for Organization, Attention and Learning Skills (GOALS) program and discuss any successes or challenges they have had when implementing these skills.

♦ Group members will learn how to organize their workspace to optimize focus and productivity.

Materials Needed

♦ GOALS binder & binder dividers
♦ *Optional:* Session 6 Fidelity Checklist (Table 6.2)
♦ Appendix 6.1: Session 6 Outline (Table 6.3)

Session Highlights

♦ Practice mindfulness (Focus on a Single Object Exercise)
♦ Check-in
  • Discuss content covered in the previous session (Prioritizing and Scheduling Tasks)
  • Review Session 5 homework (Listing and Prioritizing Tasks)
♦ Review the following skills and discuss any successes or challenges:
  • Extracting information from course syllabi
  • Effective communication
  • Contingent self-rewards
  • Taking notes
  • Time management
  • Mindfulness
  • Listing and prioritizing tasks
  • Scheduling using a planner
♦ Learn new skill
  • Workspace and course material organization

DOI: 10.4324/9781003199618-7

♦ Wrap-up
  • Summarize and review session content
  • Assign homework (organizing a course binder)
  • Discuss content covered in upcoming session

Detailed Session Content
Mindfulness Practice

Tip for Group Leaders: To facilitate internalization of the mindfulness skill, as well as provide group members with mindfulness activities for their repertoires, it is recommended that group leaders begin Sessions 6, 8, and 10 with mindfulness activities.

Exercise: Focus on a Single Object

This mindfulness exercise, along with most mindfulness exercises, is designed to help us refocus our attention on the present moment. With practice, the ability to enter a mindful state will become a powerful tool to block out distractions. For this exercise, each group member will focus on a single object of their choosing.

1. Instruct group members to choose a small object to focus on that is emotionally neutral such as a pen, pencil, book bag, item of clothing, or something similar.
2. Tell group members to notice when their mind wanders and to neutrally return their attention to the object being observed. Reassure group members that having their minds wander is not unusual and will lessen with additional practice.
3. Have group members place their selected object on the table in front of them and, without touching the object, begin to explore its surface with their eyes. Instruct group members to take time exploring what their chosen object looks like and to reflect on the different qualities that the object possesses. Examples of qualities to consider include:
   a. What does the surface of the object look like?
   b. Is it shiny or dull?
   c. Does it look smooth or rough?
   d. Does it look soft or hard?
   e. Does it have multiple colors or just one color?
   f. What else is unique about the way the object looks?
4. Tell group members to hold their object in their hand or reach out and touch the object. Ask group members to pay particular attention to the different ways their object feels. For example:
   a. Is it smooth or rough?
   b. Does it have ridges or is it flat?

    c. Is it soft or is it hard?

    d. Is it bendable or is it rigid?

    e. Does the object have areas that feel different from each other?

    f. What does the temperature of the object feel like?

    g. How much does it weigh?

    h. What else stands out about the way it feels?

Discuss

Spend a few minutes discussing group members' experiences completing this mindfulness exercise. Suggestions for group discussion include:

- Did group members notice their attention wandering during the activity?
- Did they find it difficult to neutrally refocus their attention without becoming frustrated with themselves or the task?
- What strategies did group members use to let go of distracting thoughts? Imagery (e.g., imagining thoughts floating away on the breeze)? Neutral acknowledgment (e.g., recognizing the occurrence of off-topic thoughts and purposefully shifting attention back to the neutral object)?

Check-In

- Briefly review topics covered during the last session.
  - Ask group members to summarize Session 5 (Prioritizing and Scheduling Tasks)
  - Material covered during the last session:
    - ☐ Making to-do lists and prioritizing tasks using the Important/Urgent Diagram
    - ☐ Scheduling tasks using a planner
  - Answer questions concerning the material covered during the previous session
- Homework review
  - Listing and Prioritizing Tasks—group members were asked to list tasks that needed to be completed in the upcoming week, prioritize these tasks using the Important/Urgent Diagram, and record whether or not each task was added to their calendar or planner.
  - Questions to facilitate group discussion:
    - ☐ How did prioritizing tasks impact group members' ability to get them done?
    - ☐ Any successes or difficulties encountered with completing this homework?

Skills Review

The first half of this session is devoted to problem-solving barriers that are impeding group members' successful implementation of skills that were covered in Sessions 2 through 5. A simplified chain analysis (see demonstration section) may be helpful in assisting group members to identify behaviors (e.g., avoidance) that get in the way of them making use of these skills.

Discuss

Refer to Table 6.1 to facilitate a review of skills taught at each session. Questions that may help to prompt discussion about how skills were implemented by group members are provided.

After summarizing what skills were taught at each session, ask group members to share what skills they found to be the most helpful and when and how they typically use these skills.

Table 6.1 *Skills Review—Sessions 2 through 5*

Session	Skill	Questions
Session 2: Self-Advocacy and Building Motivation	Extracting Information From Course Syllabi	♦ Has reviewing syllabi early in their courses (i.e., ideally before or after the initial class meeting) helped group members to be more prepared for class meetings and course assignments? ♦ Have group members found it helpful to add course assignments and exams listed on each syllabus to their planners? How might this strategy help facilitate planning for the completion of important coursework and the use of self-rewards?
	Effective Communication	♦ What actions have group members taken to successfully communicate with instructors this semester? ♦ What issues have come up when seeking help from instructors? ♦ Any advice from instructors that has been particularly helpful? What changes have group members made that have led to successes in the classroom?
	Contingent Self-Rewards	♦ How have group members used self-rewards to improve their motivation? ♦ What have group members done to incorporate rewards into their routines?
Session 3: Taking Notes From Lectures and Course Readings	Taking Notes	♦ How has active listening impacted group members' level of attention in class and ability to identify information needed for tests? ♦ How have group members' approach to taking notes changed, and how has it influenced the quality of their notes?

(*Continued*)

Table 6.1 (Continued)

Session	Skill	Questions
		♦ Any challenges encountered when using these note-taking strategies? How have they tackled these challenges?
Session 4: Time Awareness and Tuning Out Distractions	Time Management	♦ What changes have group members observed in their ability to judge how much time is needed to complete assignments? What could account for these changes?
	Mindfulness	♦ How have group members applied mindfulness exercises to their daily routines? What benefits have group members noticed as a result of using mindfulness? ♦ Have they encountered any difficulties when practicing mindfulness? Any suggestions of how to address these difficulties?
Session 5: Prioritizing and Scheduling Tasks	Listing & Prioritizing Tasks	♦ How have group members incorporated to-do lists into their daily or weekly routines? Have they noticed any changes as a result of using these to-do lists? ♦ What strategies have they used to prioritize tasks on their to-do lists? Have they had any difficulties with knowing what tasks to prioritize?
	Scheduling Using a Planner	♦ How have group members made use of paper or electronic planners and have they noticed any differences in their ability to keep track of events, assignments, and other important tasks? ♦ Have any challenges arisen when using a planner? How have group members attempted to overcome these challenges?

Demonstrate

Choose one or two group members who mentioned difficulties implementing a skill and perform a brief chain analysis to demonstrate how to overcome barriers to skill use. Chain analysis is a form of functional analysis with an increased focus on sequential events that led up to a specific behavior. The ultimate goal is to identify behaviors that got in the way of using a skill and to make a new plan of how to address those interfering behaviors so that the skill is used.

The following questions will help guide this process:

♦   What got in the way of using this skill? Any excuses made for putting off or not using the skill?

♦   How did the group member try to implement the skill? What was their plan of how and when to use the skill?

♦   How did this plan fail?

♦   How can this plan be revised?

♦   What might motivate the group member to complete this new plan?

Skills Introduction: Workspace and Course Material Organization

Describe

There are several advantages to organizing a workspace and class materials such as finding materials and assignments more easily, reducing stress levels, and having a neat and attractive work area that is conducive to productivity. The first step in this process is limiting both *visual and auditory distractions* in the designated workspace. Items such as pictures, interesting books, and electronics that are unrelated to the job to be done should be removed. It is also important to determine whether noise is helpful or harmful when trying to get work done and to adjust the workspace according to that preference or need.

To increase the convenience of a workspace, keep things that are most frequently used nearest at hand. This approach reduces the amount of time spent in "preparation mode" and more time will be available for studying and completing assignments. For example, it may be a good idea to keep textbooks, notebooks, binders, calculators, pencils, pens, highlighters, and sticky notes together in easily accessible locations within the workspace. These items should be kept in a specified place such as a labeled container, file drawer, or basket and should not be spread out across the surface of a workspace.

Finally, course materials should be organized as they are received. One useful way to organize notes, handouts, and other course materials is through the use of binders and binder dividers. The binder and binder dividers for each course should be clearly labeled and separate dividers should be made for the course's syllabus, lecture notes, assigned reading notes, study guides, and homework. If course materials are all electronic, a similar approach may be used by organizing course materials into specific file folders on the desktop of a computer or cloud storage platform (e.g., Google Docs, Sharepoint, and Dropbox).

Demonstrate

Lead group members through the task of reorganizing their GOALS binder and answer any questions as they come up. Handouts from the GOALS program should be ordered by session and separated by dividers for each session with an additional section for homework. Provide binder dividers and replacement handouts from the program manual if needed.

Discuss

Discuss group members' reactions to completing this activity. Some questions that could help facilitate this discussion are as follows:

♦ Why is it important to keep materials organized? Have group members ever missed an assignment because they lost papers or could not find what they needed?

♦ What makes it difficult to keep workspaces and course materials organized? How will group members apply what they learned today to get organized?

Wrap-Up

♦ Allow for questions—give group members an opportunity to ask questions about skills that were reviewed and new skills that were introduced.
♦ Session review—group leaders should briefly summarize the topics covered during the current session. Topics covered include:
  • Review of skills taught so far in the GOALS program (i.e., effective communication, contingent self-rewards, active listening, note-taking, time management, mindfulness, daily to-do lists, task prioritization, and scheduling using planners)
  • Workspace and course material organization
♦ Distribute Appendix 6.1: Session 6 Outline to group members
♦ Assign homework
  • Group members are to organize a binder for one of their classes and bring this binder with them to the next session. Use the GOALS binder as a guide on how to organize class materials.
♦ Remind group members of the next session time, place, and topics to be covered:
  • Session 7: Overcoming Procrastination and Coping with Stress
    ☐ Group members will learn strategies to overcome procrastination and deal with stressors that may hinder their success. Specifically, they will be taught how to initiate tasks, stay motivated to make progress, and use coping strategies when feeling overwhelmed.

Table 6.2 Session 6 Fidelity Checklist

Task	Rating 0	1	2
Prepared materials for the session (i.e., printed handouts for all group members and provided binder dividers)			
Completed mindfulness activity with the group			
Reviewed topics covered in the previous session			
Discussed homework assignment from the previous session			
Offered opportunity for group members to ask questions about the previous session			
Discussed skills taught in Sessions 2 through 5: ♦ Extracting information from course syllabi ♦ Effective communication ♦ Contingent self-rewards ♦ Taking notes ♦ Time management ♦ Mindfulness ♦ Listing and prioritizing tasks ♦ Scheduling using a planner			
Performed chain analysis of barriers to skill use with group member(s)			
Led group members through a reorganization of their GOALS binders			
Asked questions to assess group members' understanding of skills and to promote engagement			
Offered opportunity for group members to ask questions about the current session			
Assigned homework based on the topic covered during this session			
Mentioned date and topic of the next session			

0—Group Leader did not execute task.
1—Group Leader partially executed task.
2—Group Leader fully executed task.

Appendix 6.1: Session 6 Outline

Table 6.3 Skills Review and Reflection

Session	Skill	Points for consideration
Session 2: Self-Advocacy and Building Motivation	Extracting Information From Course Syllabi	♦ Has reviewing syllabi early in your courses (i.e., ideally before or after the initial class meeting) helped you to be more prepared for class meetings and course assignments? ♦ Have you found it helpful to add course assignments and exams listed on each syllabus to your planner? How might this strategy help you plan for the completion of important coursework and the use of self-rewards?
	Effective Communication	♦ What actions have you taken to successfully communicate with instructors this semester? ♦ Have any issues come up when seeking help? ♦ Any advice from instructors that has been particularly helpful? What changes have you made that have led to successes in the classroom?
	Contingent Self-Rewards	♦ How have you used self-rewards to improve your motivation? ♦ What have you done to incorporate rewards into your routines?
Session 3: Taking Notes From Lectures and Course Readings	Taking Notes	♦ How has active listening impacted your level of attention in class and ability to identify information needed for tests? ♦ How has your approach to taking notes changed, and how has it influenced the quality of your notes?

(Continued)

Table 6.3 (Continued)

Session	Skill	Points for consideration
		♦ Any challenges encountered when using these note-taking strategies? How have you tackled these challenges?
Session 4: Time Awareness and Tuning Out Distractions	Time Management	♦ What changes have you noticed in your ability to judge how much time is needed to complete assignments? What could account for these changes?
	Mindfulness	♦ How have you incorporated mindfulness exercises into your daily routines? What benefits have you noticed as a result of using mindfulness? ♦ Have you encountered any difficulties when practicing mindfulness? How have you tried to address these difficulties?
Session 5: Prioritizing and Scheduling Tasks	Listing & Prioritizing Tasks	♦ How have you incorporated to-do lists into your daily or weekly routines? Have you noticed any changes as a result of using these to-do lists? ♦ What strategies have you used to prioritize tasks on your to-do lists? Have you had any trouble knowing what tasks to prioritize?
	Scheduling Using a Planner	♦ How have you made use of paper or electronic planners? Have you noticed any differences in your ability to keep track of events, assignments, and other important tasks? Have you experienced any challenges using a planner? If so, what have you done to overcome them?

Organizing Your Workspace and Course Materials

Advantages of Keeping Things Organized

- ◆ Needed materials and assignments will be more easily located. As a result, much less time will be spent searching for materials and more time can be devoted to actually working toward completing assignments and study sessions!
- ◆ A neat and clean work environment contributes to reduced stress levels!
- ◆ An organized workspace means your surroundings will be more neat and attractive, which is conducive to productivity!

Tips for Organizing Your Workspace and Materials

- ◆ To increase the convenience of a workspace, *keep things that are used most frequently nearest at hand*. This strategy reduces the amount of time spent in "preparation mode" and more time will be available for studying and completing assignments.
  - Examples of items frequently needed when working on course assignments include notebooks, textbooks, binders, a calculator, pencils, pens, highlighters, and sticky notes.
- ◆ Keep items in a specific place and NOT spread out across the surface of a workspace.
  - Labeled containers, file drawers, baskets, or special boxes for storing these items may be useful.
  - Organize materials from classes as they are received.
    - □ One useful way to organize notes, handouts, and other class materials is through the use of binders and binder dividers. Refer to your GOALS binder as an example of how to organize materials from academic courses.
    - □ Electronic course materials can be organized with a similar approach. Place materials into specific file folders on your computer desktop or cloud storage platform.
- ◆ It is important that your workspace be free of visual and auditory distractors. Remove items such as pictures, interesting books, and electronics that are unrelated to the job to be done.
  - **Rule of thumb:** If something is distracting (e.g., a picture or an object), then remove it!
- ◆ Determine whether noise is helpful or harmful when trying to get work done and then adjust the workspace accordingly.

Chapter 7

Overcoming Procrastination and Coping With Stress

Quick Look

Objectives

♦ Group members will learn how to initiate tasks to ensure task completion.
♦ Group leaders will outline strategies for staying motivated to make progress.
♦ Group members will apply techniques to cope with stress and frustration.

Materials Needed

♦ Appendix 7.1: Session 7 Outline
♦ Appendix 7.2: Implementing Stress Management Techniques (Homework)
♦ *Optional:* Session 7 Fidelity Checklist (Table 7.1)

Session Highlights

♦ Check-in
   • Discuss content covered in the previous session (Workspace and Course Material Organization)
   • Review Session 6 homework (Binder organization)
♦ Learn new skills
   • Initiate tasks and stay motivated
   • Strategies for stress management
♦ Wrap-up
   • Assign homework (Implementing Stress Management Techniques)
   • Discuss content covered in the upcoming session

DOI: 10.4324/9781003199618-8

Detailed Session Content
Check-In

- ◆ Briefly review topics covered during the last session.
  - • Ask group members to summarize Session 6 (Program Review and Getting Organized)
  - • Material covered during the last session:
    - ☐ Skills learned so far during the program were reviewed, and barriers that are impeding group members' success were problem-solved.
    - ☐ How to effectively organize workspaces and course materials was also introduced and discussed.
  - • Ask group members if they have any questions concerning the material from the last session.
- ◆ Homework review
  - • Briefly discuss the homework from the last session. Group members were instructed to organize a binder for one of their classes and bring it with them to today's session.
  - • Questions to facilitate group discussion:
    - ☐ How did they organize their binders?
    - ☐ Are there any changes they have noticed since putting this organizational strategy to use?
    - ☐ What might prevent them from staying organized, and how might they overcome these challenges?

Skills Introduction: Overcoming Procrastination
Describe

Overcoming procrastination is not easy and requires a great deal of effort to achieve. In fact, nearly every part of the brain that involves executive functions plays a role in task initiation. Unfortunately, there are many external forces and distractions that make it difficult to complete a task, so it is easy to feel overwhelmed and uncertain of where to begin. However, there are several strategies that may be helpful in minimizing procrastination:

If overwhelmed→break the task down into smaller and more manageable parts

Schedule equivalent time blocks to complete each portion of the larger task. Oftentimes, task initiation is the most challenging aspect of getting things done. Once the initial steps are made to complete a task, the remaining steps become more manageable, and it is easier to make progress. It may also help to alternate between more "difficult and easy" or "boring and interesting" tasks throughout the day, which helps build momentum while taking advantage of naturally occurring breaks.

If Distracted→Use Visual Cues So Tasks Requiring Attention Cannot Be Ignored

For example, placing a textbook in plain sight on the coffee table or desk will act as a reminder to read a chapter for class. This strategy may also be used with a personal computer. For example, if a report needs to be finished, a desktop folder may be created containing all the resources needed for the project and should be placed in a prominent location on the desktop. Creating visual cues will help get the process started and act as a reminder to complete tasks once they are initiated. As discussed in the previous session, it is also useful to keep workspaces free of distractions so the possibility of getting side-tracked is minimized.

If It Is Hard To Get Started→Make Use of Rewards As a Means of Motivation

Plan a reward (and when it will be given) for the partial or full completion of a task that is difficult or unpleasant. This reward should be motivating and time-limited and not result in further procrastination. Some examples include taking a walk outside, enjoying a snack, or reading for pleasure. Enlisting a partner may also help for accountability purposes, as they can verify the task has been completed, ensure the reward is taken, and signal when it's time to resume working.

Demonstrate

Group leaders should generate examples of how to use each strategy (i.e., break down tasks, visual cues, self-rewards, task pairing, and partner up). Examples of implementing these strategies are provided below.

- Break Down Tasks—if completing a response paper to assigned readings, break the assignment down into the following tasks: reading the assigned chapters, listing out critical questions and lessons learned from the readings, making an outline, writing the paper, and proofreading it so that the paper is ready for submission.
- Visual Cues—place a sticky note in a prominent place such as a laptop to serve as a reminder to complete an on-line quiz.
- Self-Rewards—enjoy a favorite show after several hours of writing; drink a cup of coffee or tea after studying for an hour; take a bike ride or go to the gym for some exercise.
- Task Pairing—spend one hour studying for a "boring" class before spending one hour reading for an "interesting" class.
- Partner Up—schedule a "study session" with a classmate. Plan out what should be accomplished for a specified time period while working independently and what reward should be given for completing each task (e.g., ten-minute conversation with a partner).

Discuss

Ask group members to provide additional examples of how these strategies can be applied in their everyday lives.

- ♦ Where might group members encounter challenges?
- ♦ What strategies have worked for group members in the past?
- ♦ Are there other barriers that interfere with group members' ability to initiate tasks?

Skills Introduction: Stress Management

Describe

Encountering everyday stressors is inevitable and may limit productivity, as the ability to concentrate is often impaired when feeling overwhelmed or distressed. Procrastination often results from these feelings and is triggered by all the things that need to get accomplished including responsibilities and obligations outside of school. It is easy to become hyper-focused on the person, thing, or situation that is leading to stress or anxiety. In addition to the recommendations presented above, it may be helpful to use some basic stress management strategies.

Distraction by Counting (adapted from Rathus & Miller, 2014)

Counting breaths—sit in a comfortable chair, place a hand on your stomach, and take slow, deep breaths. Imagine breathing into your stomach instead of your lungs. Count how many breaths are taken before your mind wanders, then restart counting at one.

Counting by sevens—start with one hundred and subtract by seven (100, 93, 86, etc.). As this activity requires a large amount of concentration, the immediate and overwhelming feelings produced by a stressor are put on hold as thoughts are refocused elsewhere.

Distraction by Changing the Emotional State (adapted from Rathus & Miller, 2014)

- ♦ Watch one to two funny videos or look at amusing memes for one to two minutes.
  - • Laughter serves as a physical release for stress and is incompatible with feelings of distress.
- ♦ Read a letter or email from a family member or friend that relays a message of love or a sense of belongingness.
- ♦ Scroll through pictures capturing a moment of happiness or a special day.

Stressors often elicit negative or distressing emotions, so it is important to be aware of techniques that may serve to comfort and soothe the mind and body especially if the stressor is ongoing or continues to cause distress. One way to cope with distressing emotions, bring a sense of relief, and produce a calming state is to self-soothe by using the five senses. The following are examples of soothing activities that make use of each sense:

Self-Sooth by Using the Senses (adapted from Rathus & Miller, 2014)

- ◆ Smell:
  - Find a candle or incense that is pleasing to the smell, then burn it in a personal space (e.g., room and apartment)
  - Wear scented oil, perfume, or cologne that produces a feeling of happiness or confidence
  - Cook or bake food that has a pleasing smell, such as chocolate chip cookies or banana bread
- ◆ Vision:
  - Go through magazines or books and cut out pictures that are pleasing to look at or motivating. Make a collage of them to hang on the wall or carry a few in a wallet or handbag to look at away from home
  - Find a place that is soothing to look at, such as a park or garden or use a picture of a place that is soothing, such as the beach
- ◆ Hearing:
  - Listen to soothing music, such as classical, oldies, new age, etc.
  - Listen to audiobooks or podcasts on an interesting subject, such as films, music, etc.
- ◆ Taste:
  - Enjoy a favorite meal—eat slowly and savor the way it tastes
  - Carry lollipops, gum, or other small candy to eat when upset
  - Eat or drink something soothing, such as ice cream, pudding, tea, or hot chocolate. Try to eat and drink slowly so the taste can be truly enjoyed
- ◆ Touch:
  - Carry something soft or velvety to touch when needed, like a soft piece of cloth
  - Take a hot or cold shower and enjoy the feeling of water falling on the skin
  - Wear comfortable clothes, like a favorite T-shirt, baggy sweatpants, or well-worn jeans

Sometimes, it is easy to induce unnecessary stress by worrying about the future or by perseverating on the past. In both of these situations, energy is spent on passively thinking about past or upcoming stressors, but, in reality, no problem solving is actually occurring. It may be helpful to identify whether thoughts are past or future-oriented and refocus attention on the present moment.

Where Are You Now?

Tip for group leaders: It may be helpful to emphasize to group members that this skill is a form of mindfulness.

- ♦ When feeling stressed or overwhelmed, consider these questions:
  - • Where am I right now?
  - • Am I thinking about the future, worrying about something that could happen, or planning for what may happen?
  - • Am I in the past, reviewing mistakes, or reliving negative life experiences? Am I thinking about what my life could have been under different circumstances?
  - • Am I in the present moment, really paying attention to what I am doing, thinking, and feeling?
- ♦ If not in the present moment, refocus thoughts and attention on what is happening right now by following these steps:
  - • Notice what you are thinking about and recognize if you are time traveling. Bring your attention back to the present moment and focus on what is happening right now.
  - • Take slow, long breaths to help you refocus.
  - • Try to think about what you can do in the moment to make you feel better and when you are ready, how to fix the problem.

Demonstrate

Before beginning this activity, ask group members to rate their level of distress from one to ten (one = least distressed, ten = most distressed). Group members do not have to share their ratings with the rest of the group, but they should be encouraged to write them down.

Guided Imagery (adapted from Raypole, 2020)

- ♦ Sit in a comfortable, relaxed position.
- ♦ Close your eyes and begin breathing in a regular rhythm.
- ♦ Picture a place where you feel content and calm. This place may be somewhere you have previously visited, somewhere you would like to visit, or even a fictional place (e.g., beach, bedroom, or favorite park on campus).
- ♦ Use your five senses to add as much detail to the image as possible. Ask yourself: What do you hear? Can you smell any fragrances, such as pine trees, saltwater, or cookies baking in the oven? Are you warm or cool? Can you feel the air on your skin? What do you taste on your tongue? Do you see other people, or are you by yourself? Can you listen to birds singing or the gentle lap of the ocean waves on the shore?
- ♦ Continue breathing slowly as you examine the environment in your mind, continuing to check in with all five senses.
- ♦ When you are ready, slowly return from your vision. Remember where you went and remind yourself that you can go back at any time throughout your day.

After completing this activity, have group members rate their level of distress again, using the same rating scale introduced before this mindfulness activity.

Discuss

Ask group members for feedback and their impressions about the activity. Potential questions to facilitate discussion include: Did they find the exercise relaxing, helpful, or difficult to do?

What did they like or not like about the exercise? Which technique taught during this session do they think will be the most useful for them and in what situations?

Wrap-Up

- ♦ **Allow for questions**—give group members an opportunity to ask questions about the session's content
- ♦ **Session review**
  - • Topics covered during this session include:
    - ▫ Overcoming procrastination
      - – Strategies for initiating tasks (e.g., breaking down tasks, using visual cues, implementing self-rewards, task pairing, and partnering up)
    - ▫ Using stress management techniques (e.g., distraction, self-soothe, and mindfulness)
- ♦ Distribute Appendix 7.1: Session 7 outline to group members
- ♦ **Assign homework**
  - • Have group members choose and make use of two to three stress management techniques when feeling frustrated or overwhelmed during the upcoming week. Instruct group members to describe the situation that required the technique, identify what technique they used, discuss how they applied it, and evaluate its helpfulness. Distribute Appendix 7.2 to group members
- ♦ Remind group members of the next session time, place, and topics to be covered:
  - • Session 8: Planning a long-term project
    - ▫ Group members will learn how to plan a long-term project by breaking it down into smaller, more manageable tasks; prioritizing and ranking each task; and scheduling the completion of these tasks

Table 7.1 Session 7 Fidelity Checklist

Task	Rating		
	0	1	2
Prepared materials for the session (i.e., printed handouts for all group members)			
Reviewed topics covered at the previous session			
Discussed homework assignment from the previous session			
Offered opportunity for group members to ask questions about the previous session			

(Continued)

Table 7.1 (Continued)

Task	Rating		
	0	1	2
Discussed each strategy to address procrastination.			
Taught all stress management strategies to group members.			
Completed at least one practice stress management activity with group members.			
Asked questions to assess group members' understanding of skills and to promote engagement			
Offered opportunity for group members to ask questions about the current session			
Assigned homework based on the topic covered during this session			
Mentioned date and topic of the next session			

0—Group Leader did not execute task.
1—Group Leader partially executed task.
2—Group Leader fully executed task.

References

Rathus, J.H., & Miller, A.L. (2014). *DBT skills manual for adolescents.* Guilford Press.
Raypole, C. (2020, May 28). Visualization meditation: 5 exercises to try. Healthline. https://www.healthline.com/health/visualization-meditation#goals-visualization

Appendix 7.1: Session 7 Outline

Overcoming Procrastination and Coping With Stress

Overcoming Procrastination

- ♦ Just getting started with a task can be very difficult. However, once a task has been started, it is much easier to continue working on it and making progress.

Useful Strategies

- ♦ Attempting to do too much at once can make getting started even more difficult. To address this obstacle:
  - **Break tasks down** into more manageable parts
  - **Schedule equal time blocks** to complete each part of the task
- ♦ Some additional strategies for overcoming procrastination and maintaining motivation to complete them include:
  - Creating **visual cues** to serve as reminders that a task needs to be completed. Examples include placing a textbook in plain sight as a reminder to read a chapter for class and creating a desktop folder with all the resources needed for the completion of a project.
  - **Planning a reward** for partially or fully completing a task that you find hard or unpleasant to do.
  - **Alternating** between "difficult and easy" or "boring and interesting" tasks throughout the day.
  - **Partnering** with someone to complete tasks.
    - ☐ Important note: This strategy does not necessarily mean working on the task together. An example of appropriately using this strategy for assignments that must be completed independently is simply getting together with a friend or study partner and independently working on the assignment while in the same place at the same time. Working on an unpleasant or difficult activity while with another person can make the task more bearable.

Stress Management

- ♦ Learning techniques to deal with stressors is very important for maintaining self-care. It is also impossible to initiate important tasks when thinking about stressors and not focusing on the present moment. Below are some stress management techniques that may be useful:
- ♦ **Self-Distraction** is useful if one becomes hyper-focused on the person, thing, or situation that is causing the stress.

- Count your breaths—sit in a comfortable chair, put a hand on your belly, and take slow, deep breaths. Imagine breathing into your stomach instead of your lungs. Count how many breaths you take before your mind wanders, then restart your counting at one.
- Count by sevens—start with one hundred and subtract by seven (100, 93, 86, etc.). This activity requires a large amount of concentration and attention, thus it will distract you from the immediate and overwhelming feelings triggered by stress.
- Change the emotional state—watch a funny YouTube video or a clip from your favorite comedy show. A good bout of laughter will distract from the stressor and the act of laughing serves as a physical release of stress.

♦ **Self-Sooth by Using the Senses** is helpful when stress elicits distressing emotions and feelings. It is important to be aware of activities that serve to comfort and nurture when continuing to focus on stressful situations.
  - Smell (e.g., burning candles or incense, baking cookies, or preparing a favorite meal)
  - Vision (e.g., cutting out motivating pictures or images from magazines; going to the beach, park, or another favorite place that is calming)
  - Hearing (e.g., listening to soothing music, audiobooks, and podcasts)
  - Taste (e.g., enjoying a favorite meal or drink or eating something with a comforting flavor)
  - Touch (e.g., taking a hot shower or wearing your favorite comfortable t-shirt or sweatpants)

♦ **Refocusing on the Present Moment (a form of mindfulness)** is useful when one is inducing unnecessary stress by worrying about things that have not yet happened or by ruminating on things that happened in the past.
  - When feeling stressed or overwhelmed, consider these questions:
    □ Am I time-traveling to the future, worrying about something that might happen, or planning for something that might happen?
    □ Am I time-traveling to the past, reviewing mistakes, or reliving bad experiences? Or am I thinking about how my life could have been under different circumstances?
  - If not in the present moment, refocus thoughts and attention on what is happening right now by following these steps:
    □ Notice what you are thinking about and recognize if you are time traveling. Bring your attention back to the present moment and focus on what is happening in the moment. Describe the current situation to yourself.
    □ Take slow, long breaths to help you refocus and, when calm, brainstorm things that can be done to fix the problem.

Appendix 7.2: Session 7 Homework

Implementing Stress Management Techniques

Choose two stress management techniques from the session outline to use when you are feeling frustrated or overwhelmed. In the space below, describe the situation that led you to use a technique, how you applied it, and whether it was helpful.

Describe the Stressful Situation

What technique was used and how was it applied?

Was the technique helpful? Why or why not?

Describe the Stressful Situation

What technique was used and how was it applied?

Was the technique helpful? Why or why not?

Chapter 8

Planning a Long-Term Project

Quick Look

Objective

♦ Group members will learn how to plan a long-term project by dividing it into smaller, more manageable tasks (i.e., secondary and tertiary goals).

Materials Needed

♦ Appendix 8.1: Session 8 Outline
♦ Appendix 8.2: Planning a Project Worksheet (Activity and Homework; two copies per group member)
♦ *Optional:* Session 8 Fidelity Checklist (Table 8.1)

Session Highlights

♦ Check-in
  • Discuss content covered in the previous session (Overcoming Procrastination and Coping with Stress)
  • Review previous session homework (Implementing Stress Management Techniques)
♦ Learn new skill
  • Planning and execution of a long-term project
♦ Wrap-up
  • Assign homework (Planning a Project Worksheet)
  • Discuss content covered in the upcoming session

DOI: 10.4324/9781003199618-9

Detailed Session Content
Check-In

Briefly review topics covered during the previous session:

- Ask group members to summarize Session 7 (Overcoming Procrastination and Coping with Stress)
- Material covered during the last session:
  - Overcoming procrastination (e.g., breaking down tasks into manageable segments and using contingent self-rewards)
  - Coping with stress (e.g., using distraction, self-soothing, and visualization)
- Answer any questions concerning the material covered during the previous session

---

Tip for Group Leaders: As recommended in an earlier session, we suggest starting every other session with a brief mindfulness activity. This will give group members the opportunity to practice this skill while also providing a range of activity examples. Group leaders are encouraged to use whatever mindfulness activities they prefer, or they can use one of the activities provided in Appendix 4.3.

Homework Review

Group members were asked to implement two to three stress management techniques when feeling stressed or overwhelmed and to evaluate their use of these skills. Ask group members to share their experience with this exercise. The following prompts may be used to facilitate group discussion:

- Have group members describe the situation that prompted the use of each technique.
- What technique was used and how was it implemented?
- How well did the technique work to reduce stress?

Skills Introduction: Planning a Long-Term Project
Describe

This session focuses entirely on how to plan a long-term project, such as a term paper or a class presentation. Planning a long-term project relies on other skills introduced in earlier sessions, including time awareness, overcoming procrastination, prioritizing and scheduling tasks, breaking down large assignments into more manageable tasks, and improving motivation through self-reward. Given the complexity of this skill, the entire session is devoted to a thorough demonstration of its use as well as further practice applying the skill to specific examples when time permits.

Provide group members with the Planning a Project Worksheet (Figure 8.1 in Appendix 8.2) before beginning this in-session activity. Use the example of "planning a response paper" to discuss and illustrate the process of planning a long-term project.

Demonstrate

Note: an example of how to plan for the completion of a response paper is provided below. It may also be helpful to ask group members for actual class assignments that can be used for this activity in lieu of this example. The most important part of this demonstration is writing out the example on the board as it is discussed. This will help group members understand the complexity of the skill and practice using the requisite strategies, making it more likely for them to understand how to complete it in the future.

1. Identify an overarching or primary goal. Determine how many days/weeks are left before the project is due.
    a. Use a two-page response paper (i.e., reaction to two textbook chapters) for an introductory class (e.g., Introduction to Psychology) as an example.
    b. For demonstration purposes, this hypothetical response paper will be due in two weeks.
2. Break down the project into more manageable secondary goals.
    a. As this paper will be due in two weeks, solicit secondary goals from group members. (Potential responses: read the class chapters; write the paper; make revisions to the paper and prepare it for submission to the instructor.)
3. Identify materials or information needed to accomplish secondary goals.
    a. Ask group members what materials are needed to complete these secondary goals. (Potential responses: computer, textbook, access to a printer if a hard copy must be turned in.)
4. Subdivide secondary goals into tertiary goals. Again, determine what is involved in completing each task.
    a. Ask group members how they might divide the secondary goals into tertiary goals.
        i. The first goal, reading the class chapters, could be divided into (1) reading chapter one and taking notes and (2) reading chapter two and taking notes.
        ii. The second goal, writing the paper, could be divided into (1) writing a brief summary of the material, (2) writing a reaction to the material, and (3) writing a conclusion.
        iii. For the third goal, completing the paper and ensuring that it is ready for submission to the instructor, tertiary goals might include: (1) proofreading the paper, (2) submitting the paper electronically or (2) printing the paper, and (3) placing the printed copy with other course materials they always bring to class.
5. Rank secondary and tertiary goals according to priority while keeping in mind that some goals naturally come before other goals, as they build on each other.

a. With this paper (as with other assignments), some tasks naturally come before others, whereas some tasks may be interchangeable. For example, the assigned chapters of the textbook must be read before the writing of the paper can begin. With assistance from group members, group leaders should assign priority rankings to secondary and tertiary goals.

6. Assign completion dates to each secondary and tertiary goal based on priority rankings while keeping in mind when the final project is due.
   a. Ask group members to determine target dates for completing each of the secondary goals.
   b. Ask group members to determine target dates for the tertiary goals as well.

7. Instruct group members to always add scheduled secondary and tertiary goals to their planners. Advise that adjustments to their planner may be needed if some goals take longer than originally intended. By placing these due dates in their planners, they will be more likely to adhere to their plan. This planning ahead strategy will help them avoid completing a huge amount of work right before an assignment is due.

Discuss

Ask group members to identify projects to which they could apply the planning a project worksheet. Provide group members with the opportunity to ask questions concerning how to plan long-term projects using the Planning a Project Worksheet. If time permits, it may be helpful to walk through another example or have group members apply the skill on their own and then have them discuss this exercise as a group.

Wrap-Up

♦ Give group members an opportunity to ask questions about the session's content.
♦ Session review: This session focused on planning a long-term project, including a specific example of breaking down a project using the Planning a Project Worksheet.
♦ Assign homework:
   • Distribute the Planning a Project Worksheet (Appendix 8.2) and instruct group members to break up and schedule a course-related or personal long-term project. Remind group members to enter each secondary and tertiary goal into a planner, keep track of important due dates, and adhere to the intended timeline for project completion.
   • Ask group members to bring a set of notes from a recent class lecture or reading assignment
♦ Remind group members of the next session time, place, and topics to be covered.
   • In session 9, group members will learn about studying for different types of tests.

Table 8.1 Session 8 Fidelity Checklist

Task	Rating		
	0	1	2
Prepared materials for the session (i.e., printed handouts for all group members)			
Reviewed topics covered at the previous session			
Discussed homework assignment from the previous session			
Offered opportunity for group members to ask questions about the previous session			
Completed mindfulness activity with the group (optional)			
Wrote long-term planning example on the board to demonstrate the task			
Asked questions to assess group members' understanding of this skill and to promote engagement			
Assigned homework based on topic covered during this session			
Offered opportunity for group members to ask questions about the current session			
Mentioned date and topic of the next session			

0—Group Leader did not execute task.
1—Group Leader partially executed task.
2—Group Leader fully executed task.

Appendix 8.1: Session 8 Outline

Planning a Long-Term Project

Planning a Project

Skills such as time awareness, overcoming procrastination, prioritizing and scheduling tasks, and maintaining motivation through self-reward all come together when planning a long-term project. Thus, this is a complex but vital skill for success.

The Steps of Planning a Project

1. Identify the overarching or primary goal of the project and determine how many days/weeks there are to finish the project.
2. Break the project down into more manageable secondary goals.
3. Identify materials or information needed to accomplish these secondary goals.
4. Divide the secondary goals into tertiary goals and consider what is needed to complete each task.
5. Rank both secondary and tertiary goals according to priority.
   a. Keep in mind that some sub-goals naturally occur before others (e.g., chapters of a textbook must be read before a paper can be written about the content of the chapters).
6. Assign completion dates to each secondary and tertiary goal based on priority rankings. Keep in mind the due date for the final project.
7. Add scheduled goals to your planner. Some goals may take longer than originally intended, so adjust your planner as needed.

Strategies for Success

♦ Try to fit tasks like checking out a library book or visiting the writing center into daily routines so that the number of special trips taken to complete a project are minimized.
♦ Refer to the Planning a Project Worksheet completed in group as an example of how to plan an actual personal or school-related project.

Appendix 8.2: Session 8 Activity

Planning a Project Worksheet

Figure 8.1

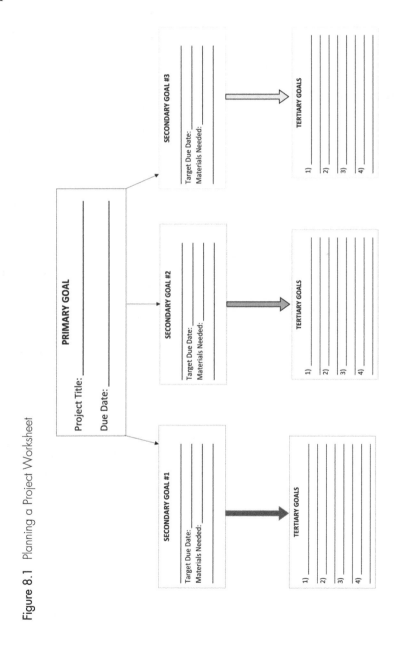

Figure 8.1 Planning a Project Worksheet

Chapter 9

Studying for Tests of Varying Formats

Quick Look

Objective

♦ Group members will learn effective strategies to study for tests, as well as format-specific approaches for different quizzes and exams.

Materials Needed

♦ Copies of notes from a recent course lecture taken by group members
♦ Appendix 9.1: Session 9 Outline
♦ Appendix 9.2: Example Practice Questions (Activity)
♦ Appendix 9.3: Practice Study Questions (Homework)
♦ *Optional:* Session 9 Fidelity Checklist (Table 9.1)

Session Highlights

♦ Check-in
  • Discuss content covered in the previous session (i.e., Planning a Long-Term Project)
  • Review assigned homework (Planning a Project Worksheet)
♦ Learn new skills
  • The "three R's of studying" and other related strategies
  • Strategies to prepare for specific test formats
♦ Wrap-up
  • Assign homework (Practice Study Questions)
  • Discuss content covered in the upcoming session

DOI: 10.4324/9781003199618-10

Detailed Session Content
Check-In

♦ Briefly review topics covered during the last session.
   • Ask group members to summarize Session 8: Planning a Long-Term Project
   • Material covered during the last session:
      ☐ Group members were taught how to break down long-term projects into secondary and tertiary goals. They were shown how to assign due dates to each goal, so that projects are completed on time.
   • Answer questions concerning the material covered during the previous session
♦ Homework review
   • Group members were asked to identify a long-term project (i.e., either a personal project or one assigned to them from a current course) and use the planning a project worksheet to divide the project into secondary and tertiary goals. Group members were also instructed to add each task to their planner or calendar, so that they meet the assignment deadline.
   • Group members were asked to bring a set of notes from a recent class lecture or reading assignment to today's session.

Skills Introduction: Studying for Tests
Describe

Test preparation capitalizes on several of the skills that were covered in previous sessions such as time management, organization, overcoming procrastination, and planning a long-term project. For example, an alternative to cramming the day before the exam is to schedule weekly study sessions to review the material as it is covered in class. However, there is not one specific way to study for a test. Rather, there are several strategies available that are outlined below. It is recommended that group members try out all strategies and retain those strategies that work best for them.

Ask group members what methods they currently use to study for tests (e.g., flash cards, quizlet/online flashcards, and/or study groups). The following questions may be used to facilitate group discussion:

♦ What study methods have group members found helpful and why?
♦ Are there any study methods they have used that have backfired? What were they and why did they not work as intended?

The study strategies described below are organized according to the "three Rs of studying": read, re-write, and review the material. This list is not exhaustive, but group members are encouraged to make use of as many strategies as possible and retain those strategies that prove to be effective.

Read

Re-read lecture and textbook notes regularly (e.g., once per week) to keep the content fresh and readily accessible. Review main ideas, patterns, and themes that emerged across each lecture or assigned reading and are likely to be on the test. For example, if studying for an abnormal psychology test, the instructor may have discussed prevalence rates, symptoms, causes, and treatments for every disorder, which may be a helpful organizational strategy to apply to prepared notes or flashcards when memorizing that information.

Re-write

Condense notes taken from lectures or course readings further by paraphrasing their content. Try to organize information according to the learning objectives provided by the instructor or course textbook. A study guide, if available, may also be a good way to reorganize notes.

Review

- ♦ Provide explicit examples of each main concept or key term as a way to apply these concepts. Oftentimes instructors will give real-world examples after defining a new concept so make sure to write these examples down.
- ♦ Study by book chapter or unit. Be sure to make use of resources available from the textbook publisher, including self-quizzes, key terms, etc.
- ♦ Use *active learning* strategies to process the information in a new way. Explain a concept to a friend or say it out loud, summarize the information in your own words, or create a diagram or concept map (i.e., a diagram that depicts suggested relationships between concepts beginning with a main idea and then branching out to show how that main idea can be broken down into specific topics) (Figure 9.1).

Tip for Group Leaders: An example concept map is provided below. It may be helpful to write this example on the board so that it is viewable to all group members.

Figure 9.1 *Example Concept Map.*

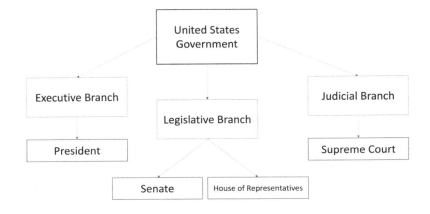

- Use mnemonics (i.e., a learning technique that aids information retention in memory) to facilitate the recall of lists and sequences of information. Listed below are different types of mnemonics often used when memorizing information:
    - Word mnemonics—the first letter of each word in a list of items is used to form another word or name that is easily remembered. Examples include:
        - Colors in the rainbow (Roy G. Biv)
        - Great Lakes (HOMES)
    - Expression mnemonics—the first letter of each item in a list is used to form another phrase that is easily remembered.
        - **Good boys do fine always** (lines in a bass clef)
        - **My very educated mother just served us nachos** (planets in the solar system)
    - Music mnemonics—important words or items are inserted into song lyrics. This method tends to work best with longer lists. Examples include:
        - ABC song
        - "Days of the week" (set to the Addams family theme song)

Strategies for Specific Test Formats

Multiple-Choice Questions

- Write multiple choice questions using the learning objectives, key terms, and definitions from the course textbook or from the lecture.
- Develop paper or electronic flashcards of key terms and definitions.
- Create multiple-choice questions that *apply* the concepts taught in class. For instance, create a multiple-choice question that asks for a real-world example that best illustrates the concept and the four answer choices represent potential examples of that concept. Helpful tip: the best example of this concept may have been given in class or may be retrieved from the textbook.

Short-Answer and Essay Questions

- Develop outlines to answer hypothetical questions that are derived from the main themes presented in class lectures. Oftentimes, exam questions come from unit or book chapter summaries or lecture learning objectives. Instructors may also make use of essay questions found in the review sections of the course textbook.
- A common type of question format used by instructors is having students take one side of an argument or debate (e.g., nature vs. nurture in an abnormal psychology class) where students provide supporting evidence for each side or compare and contrast two related concepts.
- Concept maps (discussed above) are also helpful in preparing for short answer and essay questions, as they provide a visual representation of how ideas or terms relate to one another.

Demonstrate

Distribute the Example Practice Questions handout (Appendix 9.2) to group members. Group leaders should discuss the example questions and link them to the information provided earlier in the session. Then, instruct group members to develop a concept map or mnemonic based on the notes they had taken during a recent course lecture. Lastly, group members should develop one exam question derived from these lecture notes.

Discuss

Allow group members the opportunity to share how they applied one of the active learning strategies (i.e., concept map or mnemonic) to the notes they brought with them. Then, ask them to share the exam question they created from these notes. Have a group discussion concerning how group members plan to use these study strategies when preparing for an upcoming exam.

Tip for Group Leaders: It may be helpful to print out a copy of the example note-taking passage from Session 3 (Appendix 3.2) in case group members forget to bring a copy of their personal notes.

Additional questions to prompt group discussion include:

♦ What study strategies do group members plan to use to prepare for an up-coming exam?
♦ What barriers might arise when they use these study strategies for actual exams and how might they address these barriers?
♦ What approach did they use when developing exam questions for this activity?

Wrap-Up

♦ **Allow for questions:** Give group members an opportunity to ask questions about the material covered in session.
♦ **Session Review:** Topics covered during this session included:
  • Using the "three R's of studying" and other active learning strategies
  • Developing practice questions for specific test formats
♦ **Homework:** Distribute Practice Study Questions (Appendix 9.3) to group members. Group members are to develop study questions from a course lecture that they attend in the upcoming week. Specifically, they will write two multiple-choice questions, one short answer question, and one essay question, and then provide answers to these questions using their course materials (e.g., lecture notes and textbooks).

♦   Remind group members of the next session time, place, and topics to be covered.
  •   Group members will review skills learned throughout the duration of the GOALS program and complete end-of-program paperwork to assess their progress.

Table 9.1 Session 9 Fidelity Checklist

Task	Rating		
	0	1	2
Prepared materials for the session (i.e., printed handouts for all group members)			
Reviewed topics covered at the previous session			
Discussed homework assignment from the previous session			
Offered opportunity for group members to ask questions about the previous session			
Drew two to three examples of study strategies on the board (e.g., mnemonics, concept map)			
Practiced several strategies for different testing formats			
Asked questions to assess group members understanding of this skill and to promote engagement			
Offered opportunity for group members to ask questions about the current session			
Assigned homework based on the topic covered during this session			
Mentioned date and topic of the next session			

0—Group Leader did not execute task.
1—Group Leader partially executed task.
2—Group Leader fully executed task.

Appendix 9.1: Session 9 Outline

Studying for Tests of Varying Formats

General Test Preparation Strategies

Read
♦ Reread lecture and textbook notes regularly (e.g., once per week) to keep the content fresh and readily accessible.
♦ Review main ideas, patterns, and themes that emerged across each lecture or assigned reading and that are likely to be on the test.

Re-write
♦ Condense notes taken from lectures or course readings further by paraphrasing their content.
♦ Try to organize information according to the learning objectives provided by the instructor or course textbook.
♦ If available, use a study guide to reorganize notes.

Review
♦ Provide explicit examples of each main concept or key word as a way to apply these concepts.
♦ Study by book chapter or unit. Be sure to make use of resources available from the textbook publisher, including self-quizzes, key terms, etc.
♦ Use *active learning* strategies to process the information in a new way. Explain a concept to a friend or say it out loud, summarize the information in your own words, or create a diagram or concept map (i.e., a diagram that depicts suggested relationships between concepts beginning with a main idea and then branching out to show how that main idea can be broken down into specific topics).
♦ Use mnemonics (i.e., a learning technique that aids information retention in memory) to facilitate the recall of lists and sequences of information (e.g., Roy G. Biv = Colors in the rainbow; **G**ood **b**oys **d**o **f**ine **a**lways = lines in a bass clef).

Strategies for Specific Test Formats

It is helpful to know as much as possible about the test format (e.g., multiple-choice, short answer, and essay questions) before preparing for a test, as this might inform what study strategies are employed. Ask the instructor about the format of the test and use the provided study guides, syllabus, lecture notes, and study partners to predict and develop possible exam questions in the format that will be used by the instructor. It is also a good idea to practice answering these questions using the same time limits that will be set by the instructor for the actual exam.

Multiple-Choice Questions

- ♦ Write multiple choice questions using the learning objectives, key terms, and definitions from the course textbook or from the lecture.
- ♦ Develop paper or electronic flashcards of key terms and definitions.
- ♦ Create multiple-choice questions that *apply* the concepts taught in class. An example is a multiple-choice question that asks for a real-world example that best illustrates the concept and the four answer choices represent potential examples of that concept. Helpful tip: the best example of this concept may have been given in class or may be retrieved from the textbook.

Short-Answer and Essay Questions

- ♦ Develop outlines to answer hypothetical questions that are derived from the main themes presented in class lectures. Oftentimes, exam questions come from unit or book chapter summaries or lecture learning objectives. Instructors may also make use of essay questions found in the review sections of the course textbook.
- ♦ A common type of question format used by instructors is having students take one side of an argument or debate (e.g., nature vs. nurture in an abnormal psychology class) where students provide supporting evidence for each side or compare and contrast two related concepts.
- ♦ Concept maps (discussed above) are also helpful in preparing for short answer and essay questions, as they provide a visual representation of how ideas or terms relate to one another.

Appendix 9.2: Session 9 Activity

Example Practice Questions

Multiple-Choice Questions

Which of the following are considered active learning strategies?

    A. Explaining the concept to a friend
    B. Summarizing the content in your own words
    C. Creating a concept map
    D. All of the above

Short Answer Question

Why is it helpful to review your notes each day, rather than only studying them in preparation for a test?

Essay Question

Compare and contrast current study methods to the study methods that were described in this session.

Appendix 9.3: Session 9 Homework

Practice Study Questions

Based on a recent lecture given in one of your courses, develop two multiple-choice questions, one short answer question, and one essay question, then provide answers to these questions using your course materials (e.g., lecture notes and textbook).

1. **Briefly summarize (1–2 sentences) the lecture from which you are developing your practice study questions.**

   _____
   _____
   _____

2. **Two multiple-choice questions:**
   Question:
      a.
      b.
      c.
      d.
   Answer:
   Question:
      a.
      b.
      c.
      d.
   Answer:

3. **One short answer question:**
   Question:

   Answer:

4. **One essay question:**

   Question:

   Answer:

Chapter 10

Summary of Program and Progress Made

Quick Look

Objectives

- ◆ Review skills that were taught at each session and ask questions that will prompt discussion about how these skills were used by group members.
- ◆ Discuss the progress group members have made and how they will continue to use the skills they have learned to reach their life goals.

Materials Needed

- ◆ *Optional:* Session 10 Fidelity Checklist (Table 10.1)
- ◆ *Optional*: Progress Monitoring Measures

Session Highlights

- ◆ Practice mindfulness
- ◆ Check-in
  - • Discuss content covered in the previous session (Studying for Tests of Varying Formats)
  - • Review Session 9 Homework (Practice Study Questions)
- ◆ Review skills and discuss progress
  - • Extracting information from course syllabi
  - • Effective communication
  - • Contingent self-rewards
  - • Taking notes
  - • Time management
  - • Mindfulness
  - • Listing and prioritizing tasks
  - • Scheduling using a planner
  - • Getting organized
  - • Overcoming procrastination
  - • Stress management

DOI: 10.4324/9781003199618-11

- Planning projects
- Studying for tests
◆ Wrap-up
  - Allow time for group members to ask any remaining questions
  - Distribute progress monitoring measures (Optional)
  - Congratulate group members for program completion

Detailed Session Content

Tips for Group Leaders: As recommended in earlier sessions, we suggest starting every other session with a brief mindfulness activity. This will give group members the opportunity to practice this skill while also providing a range of activity examples. Group leaders are encouraged to use whatever mindfulness activities they prefer, or they may use one of the activities provided in Appendix 4.3.

Check-In

- ◆ Briefly review topics covered during the previous session.
  - Ask group members to summarize Session 9.
  - Material covered during the last session:
    - □ Approaches to studying for tests of varying formats (e.g., multiple-choice, short answer, and essay)
  - Answer any questions about the material covered during the last session.
- ◆ Homework review
  - Group members were instructed to develop practice study questions based on a recently attended lecture of a current course.
  - Questions to facilitate group discussion:
    - □ What strategies did group members use to develop study questions? Did they experience any challenges when attempting to develop study questions? If so, how did they address these challenges?
  - Using effective study strategies is crucial to student success, and it is important that group leaders allow sufficient time to problem-solve any challenges group members may have had when implementing the skills reviewed in Session 9.
    - □ Encourage group members to share any barriers that got in the way of using the studying strategies taught during the previous session. Choose one or two group members who mentioned difficulties and perform a brief chain analysis to demonstrate how to overcome these barriers. The following questions will help facilitate chain analysis:

- How did the group member try to implement the skill? What was their plan of how and when to use the skill? For example, were all materials given by instructors read, rewritten, and reviewed?
- How did this plan fail?
- How can this plan be revised?
- What might motivate the group member to complete this new plan (e.g., self-rewards or accountability from a study partner)?

Skills Review

The remainder of the session is devoted to reviewing the skills covered in Sessions 2 through 9, allowing group members to reflect on their skill use, and answering any remaining questions that group members may have.

Discuss

Refer to Table 10.2 to facilitate a review of the skills taught at each session. Questions that may help to prompt discussion about how skills were implemented by group members are provided. Encourage group members to reflect on the progress they have made over the course of the GOALS program, to discuss ways in which skill use has been beneficial to them, and to share any useful strategies they have used while learning to implement these skills.

Wrap-Up

- Provide group members with a final opportunity to ask any remaining questions they may have about the material covered during the GOALS program.
- Distribute progress measures (optional).
- Congratulate group members on successfully completing the program and remind them to reward themselves for all their hard work!

Table 10.1 Session 10 Fidelity Checklist

Task	Rating		
	0	1	2
Prepared materials for the session (Note: progress measures are optional)			
Completed mindfulness activity with the group (optional)			
Reviewed topics covered at the previous session			
Discussed homework assignment from the previous session			

(*Continued*)

Table 10.1 (Continued)

Task	Rating		
	0	**1**	**2**
Offered opportunity for group members to ask questions about the previous session			
Discussed skills taught in Sessions 2 through 9: ♦ Extracting information from course syllabi ♦ Effective communication ♦ Contingent self-rewards ♦ Taking notes ♦ Time management ♦ Mindfulness ♦ Listing and prioritizing tasks ♦ Scheduling using a planner ♦ Getting organized ♦ Overcoming procrastination ♦ Stress management ♦ Planning projects ♦ Studying for tests			
Asked questions to assess group members' understanding of skills and to promote engagement			
Offered opportunity for group members to ask final questions about GOALS program material			

0—Group Leader did not execute task.
1—Group Leader partially executed task.
2—Group Leader fully executed task.

Appendix 10.1: Skills Review: Sessions 2 through 9

Table 10.2 Skills Review: Sessions 2 through 9

Session	Skill	Questions
Session 2: Self-Advocacy and Building Motivation	Extracting Information From Course Syllabi	◆ Has reviewing syllabi early in their courses (i.e., ideally before or after the initial class meeting) helped group members to be more prepared for class meetings and course assignments? ◆ Have group members found it helpful to add course assignments and exams listed on each syllabus to their planners? How might this strategy help facilitate planning for the completion of important coursework and the use of self-rewards?
	Effective Communication	◆ What actions have group members taken to communicate with instructors this semester? ◆ What issues have come up when seeking help from their instructors? ◆ Any advice from instructors that has been particularly helpful? What changes have group members made that have led to successes in the classroom?
	Contingent Self-Rewards	◆ How have group members used self-rewards to improve their motivation? ◆ What have group members done to incorporate rewards into their routines?

(Continued)

Table 10.2 (Continued)

Session	Skill	Questions
Session 3: Taking Notes From Lectures and Course Readings	Taking Notes	♦ How has active listening impacted group members' level of attention in class and ability to identify information needed for tests? ♦ How have group members' approach to taking notes changed and how has it influenced the quality of their notes? ♦ Any challenges encountered when using these note-taking strategies? How have they tackled these challenges?
Session 4: Time Awareness and Tuning Out Distractions	Time Management	♦ What changes have group members observed in their ability to judge how much time is needed to complete assignments? What could account for these changes?
	Mindfulness	♦ How have group members applied mindfulness exercises to their daily routines? What benefits have they noticed as a result of using mindfulness? ♦ Have group members encountered any difficulties with practicing mindfulness? Any suggestions of how to address these difficulties?
Session 5: Prioritizing and Scheduling Tasks	Listing & Prioritizing Tasks	♦ How have group members incorporated to-do lists into their daily or weekly routines? Have group members noticed any changes as a result of using these to-do lists? ♦ What strategies have they used to prioritize tasks on their to-do lists? Have they had any difficulties with knowing what tasks to prioritize?

(Continued)

Table 10.2 (Continued)

Session	Skill	Questions
	Scheduling Using a Planner	♦ How have group members made use of paper or electronic planners? Have they noticed any differences in their ability to keep track of events, assignments, and other important tasks? ♦ Have any challenges arisen when using a planner? How have group members attempted to overcome these challenges?
Session 6: Program Review and Getting Organized	Getting Organized	♦ What changes have group members made to their workspace to improve organization and lessen distractions? ♦ What other strategies have they used to stay organized?
Session 7: Overcoming Procrastination and Coping With Stress	Overcoming Procrastination	♦ What strategies have worked well for group members to overcome procrastination and initiate tasks? ♦ What strategies have helped group members maintain their motivation to make progress on tasks? ♦ What barriers have they encountered when trying to use these strategies? How have they addressed them?
	Stress Management	♦ What stress management techniques have group members used, and how have they been useful? Which techniques do they plan to use in the future? ♦ What barriers have group members experienced when trying to use stress management techniques and how have they addressed them?

(Continued)

Table 10.2 (Continued)

Session	Skill	Questions
Session 8: Planning a Long-Term Project	Planning Projects	♦ How have group members used the planning a project worksheet to complete long-term projects? ♦ How well were group members able to keep to the timeline they outlined on this worksheet? ♦ Did group members use any additional skills (e.g., contingent self-rewards) to stay on track?
Session 9: Studying for Tests of Varying Formats	Studying for Tests	♦ What study strategies have group members used when preparing for tests? ♦ How have group members' approach to studying changed depending on the test format? ♦ What challenges have come up when using these study strategies? How have group members overcome these challenges?

Index

Page numbers in italics indicate figures.

T - #0077 - 090625 - C0 - 280/210/9 - PB - 9781032058764 - Matt Lamination